Coaching Defensive Line Play

Kenny Ratledge

COACHES CHOICE™

ISBN: 978-1-60679-137-0
Library of Congress Control Number: 2010940165
Cover design: Brenden Murphy
Book layout: Studio J Art & Design
Front cover photo: ©J. Meric/Getty Images

Coaches Choice
P.O. Box 1828
Monterey, CA 93942
www.coacheschoice.com

Dedication

I would like to dedicate this book to my family.

Thanks to Debbie, Patrick, and Laura for all your support.

Acknowledgments

I would like to thank Darlene Metcalf for typing the manuscript and official Lee Hedrick for reviewing the rules included in the book.

I would also like to thank Vernon Chandler and Stan Webber of Coach's Office for their invaluable help with the diagrams.

Contents

Introduction

Who in the coaching profession has not heard—or used—tired old clichés such as *"games are won or lost in the trenches," "they need to dominate the line of scrimmage," "they have to stop the run,"* or *"the defense must generate a pass rush"*? The fact of the matter is that these clichés are true: a defense—to be successful—*must* win at the line of scrimmage and in the trenches, *must* be able to stop the run, and *must* apply pressure to the quarterback. The defensive line is the focal point of the defense's attempt to reach these goals.

Defensive linemen constitute the first stopping point of the defense. The defensive line has the crucial responsibility of controlling the line of scrimmage and pressuring the quarterback. The defensive line sets the temperament of the total defense. Failure to uphold prescribed duties results in other defensive assets being channeled to, or near, the line of scrimmage. Dilution of other units to strengthen the line, obviously, can cause glaring weaknesses in other areas, such as pass coverage. Deficiencies in the defensive line can result in:

- Explosive plays (long runs/passes)
- Lost gap integrity
- Forcing defensive backs to get involved in defending the run game (This eight-men-in-the-box philosophy weakens deep coverage.)
- Having no effective pass rush (which hangs defensive backs out to dry)
- Linemen being knocked back into linebackers who are unable to scrape downhill to the attack point
- A jailbreak by offensive linemen to the second level because defensive linemen can be blocked one-on-one
- A domino effect (If the line is inept other units are put under tremendous pressure.)

Effective defensive line play results in:
- Being able to play seven men in the box thus strengthening deep coverage (The University of Miami Hurricanes and the Tampa Bay Buccaneers, in their heyday, are two prime examples of a strong front seven.)
- The ball being pushed to the perimeter

- The offense becoming one-dimensional (If they can't run they will have to throw the ball. The advantage goes to the defense in this scenario.)
- Breaking the offense's will (If they can't run the ball, offenses start to panic.)

There has never been a dominant defense that wasn't strong up front. Strong defensive line play is the stuff of legends. NFL football lore is replete with mythical defensive line units.

Any educated fan has heard of legendary line units such as the 1970s Minnesota Vikings' "Purple People Eaters," composed of Gary Larsen, Alan Page, Jim Marshall, and Carl Eller. These men helped lead the Vikings to four Super Bowl appearances. Another example is the "Fearsome Foursome" of the Los Angeles Rams, manned by Deacon Jones, Merlin Olsen, Rosey Grier, and Lamar Lundy. The Miami Dolphins' "No Names" defensive line made up of Manny Fernandez, Bob Heinz, Bill Stanfill, and Vern Den Herder set the NFL record of 17-0 in 1972. My personal favorite was the "Steel Curtain" of the four-time Super Bowl champion Pittsburgh Steelers with "Mean" Joe Greene, Dwight White, L.C. Greenwood, and Ernie Holmes anchoring the defense.

This book explores all the different elements of defensive line play. Most of the information on defensive line play on the market today is tucked away in a few paragraphs in a few coaching manuals. This body of work explores everything from philosophy of line play to mental and physical qualifications, intangibles, alignments, fundamentals, blocking schemes, and stunts, to name a few. An exhaustive list of drills is also included. This information can be used no matter the style or alignment structure you use. It can be used by coaches who subscribe to even or odd front philosophies.

1

Philosophy of
Defensive Line Play

Two schools of thought prevail today on the style of defensive line play: the two-gap theory and the one-gap theory. The two-gap theory places defensive linemen in a head-up position on offensive linemen and asks them to defend the gaps on either side of the blocker. In essence, they are responsible for two gaps on alignment.

Many two-gap defenses base out of a 3-4 concept. At the snap, defensive linemen are asked to control and knock back the offensive man and play the gap to the playside. Obviously, defensive linemen who are asked to take this approach must possess physical qualities of size and strength. Defenses which subscribe to this style of play rely on patience, balance, and simplicity to slow down the offense.

This bend-but-don't-break philosophy emphasizes a simple and sound attitude. However, to the offense it is hard to distinguish which linebackers are designated as rushers and which ones will drop into coverage in a 3-4 structure. Also, teams that run a lot of "check with me" plays—especially option teams—have recognition problems when defensive gap responsibilities are not well defined.

In the two-gap system, linebackers overlap. They adjust on the run to what they see as they work downhill. Linebackers fit where linemen aren't. Many two-gap defenses play zone coverage with a minimum amount of man-to-man coverage.

Since two-gap defenses are usually conservative in nature, they have problems creating big plays, such as tackles for a loss, sacks, quarterback pressures, and turnovers. An effective pass rush on the quarterback is difficult from a head-up position.

Vince Lombardi subscribed to the bend-but-don't-break theory with great results. He advocated a concave look for his defensive line. He felt the ends should be positioned on the line of scrimmage but the tackles should be flexed off the ball. He coached his tackles to align 18 inches off the ball except on short yardage. Lombardi felt the cushion allowed his tackles the added room to read and react to the blocking scheme. Tom Landry fathered the flex defense with the Dallas Cowboys. This lateral emphasis of line play became the rage.

The antithesis of this theory pioneered by the Miami Hurricanes and Dallas Cowboys is the pressure-oriented one-gap concept. This style of play allows defenses to use smaller, more athletic players because they only have to control one gap—or side—of an offensive lineman. A defender who is placed on the edge of an offensive lineman doesn't need as much bulk and strength as a head-up two-gap defender. Therefore, this style of play allows defenses to be successful with players of limited ability.

Penetrating defenses can make effective use of undersized players. Edge defenders are in a better position to penetrate and pressure the offense. Each gap has a specific defender assigned to that particular gap, allowing for multiple looks, which cause the offense recognition problems. Defensive multiplicity stresses offensive blocking schemes. While two-gap defenses are simple and sound, one-gap defenses are multiple and sound. The one-gap system allows for better disguise, stems, or move-to alignments.

Most one-gap designs read on the run. Defenders read the blocking scheme as they attack. Two-gap defensive linemen must attack an offensive man, while one-gap linemen attack their gapside shade of the offensive man. You are either throwing or catching. One-gap teams prefer to throw. Big plays such as minus-yardage hits, turnovers, sacks, and pressures are the result of this aggressive attacking style. Pass rush and coverage will be greatly enhanced by the vertical nature of line play. Another huge advantage of one-gap play over two-gap responsibilities is that one-gap is more enjoyable to play.

Both styles of play have inherent advantages and disadvantages, but the prevalent style of play today is the vertical upfield pressure one-gap style. Both techniques are explored in this book.

2

Qualifications

In football, as in any other sport, requirements and qualities differ according to the position played. For example, baseball coaches look for particular attributes from infielders that might not necessarily be effective in an outfielder. By the same token, basketball teams look for skills in a guard that might not be desired in a power forward or center. This chapter will enumerate the mental, physical, and intangible qualifications that are crucial in a defensive lineman.

Just as differing skills are needed between groups of similar positional players, such as infielders in baseball, disparate skills are needed within defensive groups. For example, skills needed to play defensive end, in a given defensive system, may be dissimilar from defensive tackle.

Mental Qualifications

Mental Toughness

Defensive linemen take a pounding play after play. There are no plays that allow them to go through the motions. The next play might be a running play where the offensive lineman hits them in the mouth, or a pass play that requires the lineman to rush the quarterback.

Few defensive linemen—after the first few games—are 100 percent healthy. Defensive linemen are always banged up. It may be nothing serious but the continuous contact does take a toll after a while.

It takes a mentally tough individual to play through the aches and pains. Defensive linemen don't miss a game because of a tight hamstring or a strained oblique muscle as they do in some other sports.

Fiercely Competitive

To be an effective defensive lineman a player must be a fighter who accepts the one-on-one combat challenge. Who is the better man? Defensive linemen must take pride in hand-to-hand combat with any and all comers. He is the Marine of defensive football.

The defensive line is under attack each and every play. No other defensive position on the football field has contact on every play. It takes a special type of player to mentally handle the 50 to 60 plays that require contact every game.

Most offensive coaches start with the defensive line when diagramming a passing or running play. They first block the line, then progress vertically to the linebacker and secondary units. Offensive coaches know they must first neutralize the defensive line to have a successful play.

Unselfish

The defensive line—like the offensive line in many respects—has recognition problems. Defensive linemen may not get the acclaim afforded to other positions. As a result, defensive linemen must be self-motivated and take pride in the fact that they and their coaches know when they do a good job.

Defensive linemen must put the team first. Individual goals must be secondary. Linemen understand they must defend their assigned gap responsibility for the defense to be successful. Freelancing can leave a gap unfilled, which could result in a big play for the offense.

An effective defensive lineman must be a total player. He must have the discipline to play run or pass. Some individuals only want to rush the quarterback. They don't want to do the grunt work. These players are a liability to the defense.

Concentration

Defensive linemen must be able to concentrate on their assignment for each play. There is no room for mental errors.

Mental errors arise through a lack of concentration and a lackadaisical attitude during the week and lead to big plays for the offense on game days. One mental mistake from a defensive lineman can give the offense a touchdown or field goal. Mental mistakes can also keep a drive alive and give more time of possession and better field position to an opponent.

Self-pride is a great way to avoid mental errors. Effective defenders refuse to allow *anything* to disturb or distract their concentration. Lack of concentration caused by fatigue is the coach's fault.

Consistency

A player can't be great if he is up and down from day to day or week to week. The effective player will discipline himself to be consistent every day and every week.

Players who habitually work hard to improve will be better than consistent—they will be consistently better. The old saying *"you play like you practice"* is true. Players must be encouraged to develop good habits.

A coach can foster consistency. An effective coach—like an effective player—doesn't take days or practices off. Coaches must lead by example. They need to demand that players give coaches *their* best each day as coaches give players *their* best.

Recognition

Former NFL coach Buddy Ryan's definition of great defense is to play run when a run play has been called, and play pass when a pass has been called. Obviously, his comment is tongue-in-cheek, but there is a lot of truth to the observation.

If the defense can read or recognize the cues given by the offense, it has a good chance to defeat the play. What better position to notice these cues than the defensive line? Pre-snap keys, line splits, line depths, and stances serve to give insight on the play. Today's offensive linemen are so big in many cases that they must cheat in their stances to get where they are going more quickly. As a result, they cheat in their stances more than any other position in football.

Not only do defensive linemen need recognition skills on the line of scrimmage but they need to recognize the tactical situation. These skills are developed through film study, tip sheets, and effective defensive game planning. Defensive linemen who recognize the tactical situation are obviously more effective than those who have no idea about the situation.

Recognition skills allow defenders to understand the contingency situation. How much time is remaining? What is the down-and-distance, or field zone? What is the formation? What plays do they like in this formation? Is it a four-minute or two-minute situation? Is it a reactive situation? (For example, what does the offense like to do on first down after a first down rushing, on first down after a first down passing the ball, on first down after an explosive run, or on first down after an explosive pass?)

Physical Qualifications

The ideal defensive lineman has the size and strength to stuff the run and the speed and athleticism to rush the quarterback. He is able to play both run and pass equally well. If you have a defensive lineman with such physical qualities, consider yourself blessed. These All-American types are few and far between.

Most productive players fit into one of two categories. The first category is the big, physical type of player who is a space eater. These guys eat up blocks because of ample girth and ballast. They are very effective in keeping offensive linemen off linebackers and in holding a point. These linemen play with leverage and a good base. They cannot be knocked off the line of scrimmage, sideways, or off balance. They are very effective lateral-type players. In essence, they are effective run stuffers. However, they are not proficient at getting vertical or applying pressure on the quarterback.

The second type of defensive lineman is the antithesis of the run stuffer. He is a disrupter. He relies on quickness and explosiveness. He specializes in vertical pushes. He is blessed with great closing speed. He is a slasher who makes plays deep in the backfield. A major drawback for this type of player is that he may find it difficult to hold a point.

No matter an individual's forte, coaches should expect some basic physical characteristics or aptitudes from each player. They include:
- The ability to react quickly because of the close proximity to offensive players (Defensive linemen don't have the luxury of watching a play develop before reacting.)
- Low pad level (The ability to use big muscle groups is crucial.)
- Explosive strength (which is needed to separate and disengage)
- An understanding of leverage
- Quick hands and feet
- Above-average hand/arm strength (Defensive linemen are involved in grabbing, turning, and throwing motions.)
- Lateral quickness in a small area
- Flexibility (which facilitates proper leverage)
- Willingness to refine God-given skills
- Commitment to playing hard each snap

Defensive linemen are universally divided into tackle or end subgroups. Following are some desired traits and strengths each group should possess. Also included are coaching strategies to take advantage of each group's strengths.

Tackle

Tackles ideally possess:
- Great peripheral vision (Unlike ends that mainly face blocks coming inside-out, tackles are attacked from all angles.)
- Shorter, more powerful physiques
- The ability to get a push on guards (They should be able to collapse the pocket.)
- Bull or power-type pass rush skills (They should have in their toolbox such pass rush moves as push-pull, rips, clubs, and spins.)

End

Ends ideally possess:
- Quickness to cover ground quickly (Elite speed will allow the rusher to get his shoulder past the offensive tackle's shoulder.)
- Closing speed to the quarterback
- Enough wingspan to be able to use an assortment of pass rush moves and be able to knock down passes
- Stamina to be able to rush the quarterback all game long
- Enough upper body strength to execute counter moves when the initial pass rush move has been nullified
- Enough physicality to play base blocks and not be turned out and have the discipline not to run around base blocks

It is logical to place the best run player to the strongside (tight end) with a flip-flop assignment, or to the defense's left. It is also advantageous to align the best pass rushing end to the quarterback's blind spot, away from the tight end, or to the defense's right.

Intangibles

Good coaching and preparation will serve to prepare for all the contingencies that can happen in a game. However, some players have intangibles that are usually God-given. The really special players have a sixth sense when it comes to sniffing out particular types of plays. Effective coaching can refine this instinct to some extent but for the most part these players bring this inherent ability to the table. Players may have an instinctive feel for diagnosing quickly whether a particular play is a run or pass. Or they may have a knack for sniffing out screens, draws, or trick plays. They may have a high degree of awareness of line splits, offensive stances, or other offensive mannerisms that may tip off the upcoming play. Or they may have a unique ability to anticipate the snap count—a trait that is highly valued by defensive coaches because it allows the defender to jump the snap count and disrupt the opponent's offense. Many of these intangibles can be cultivated and used by the defensive line coach.

3

Alignments

Some teams like to play vanilla fronts and coverages, and subscribe to the theory that it is best to be simple and execute. Teams which follow this creed need more talent than the other team or they are in trouble.

Offenses have the advantage when they know where defensive players will line up. They can confidently plan their run and pass blocking schemes because they know where everyone will be.

Other teams choose multiplicity, preferring the offense not know where, or how, they will line up. Teams can be successful when they build a good base and expand from there—without overloading the players. Teams don't have to make radical changes to be multiple. Larry New, a former assistant coach with Kentucky and Alabama, stated that when a player moves six inches he has created a new front.

Multiple fronts allow defenses to:
- Respond to multiple offenses
- Take advantage of the best features of various defensive systems (e.g., 4-3, 5-2, split 4, 46, etc.)
- Appear complicated to offenses
- Cover any—and all—offensive linemen (No offensive lineman has the luxury of being uncovered all the time. Multiple fronts press and stress each offensive lineman.)
- Stem or move fronts

- Take advantage of down-and-distance situations
- Attack hash tendencies
- Control line splits
- Align defensive strengths on offensive weaknesses
- Hide weaknesses in personnel

Common Defensive Fronts

Even Fronts

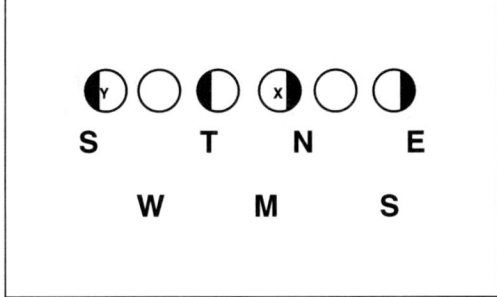

Figure 3-1. Over

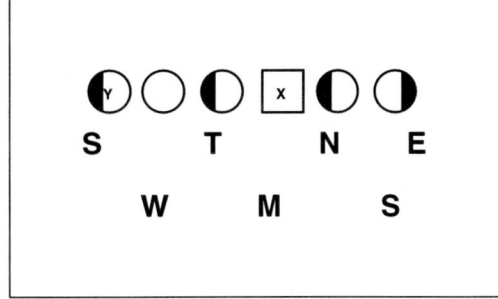

Figure 3-2. Over G

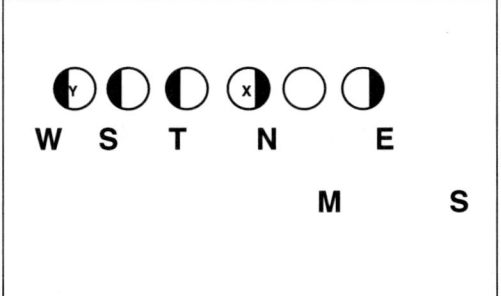

Figure 3-3. Slide

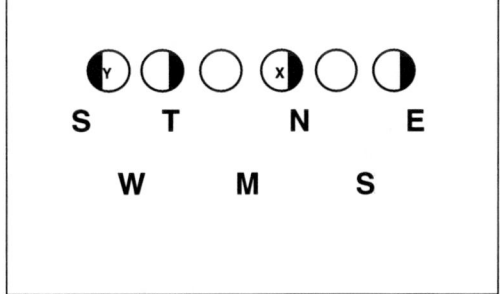

Figure 3-4. Wide

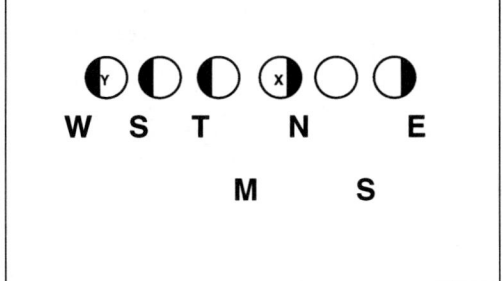

Figure 3-5. Solid

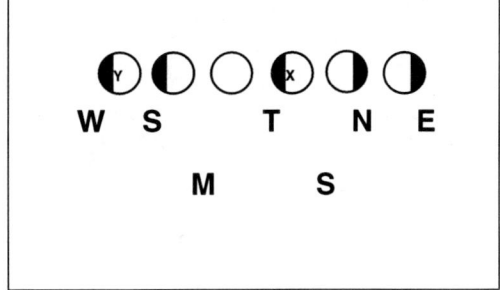

Figure 3-6. Under

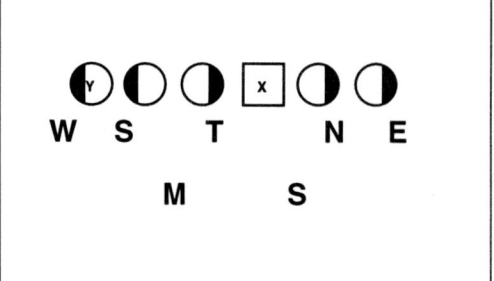

Figure 3-7. Under G

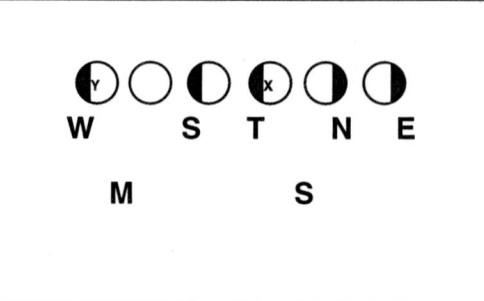

Figure 3-8. Diamond

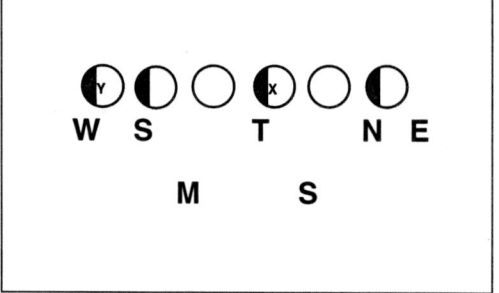

Figure 3-9. Wide under

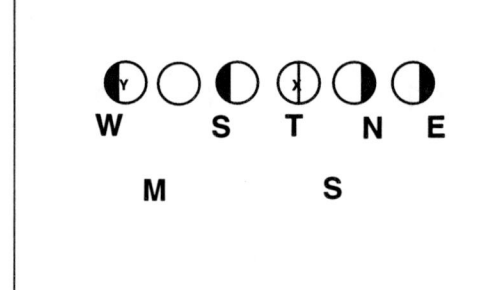

Figure 3-10. Cowboy

Odd Fronts

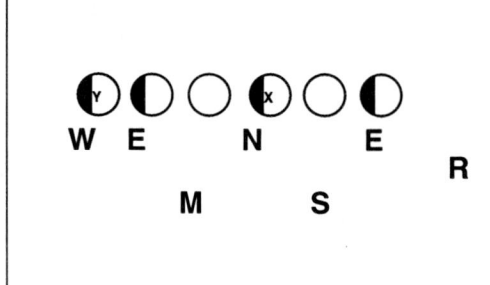

Figure 3-11. Okie

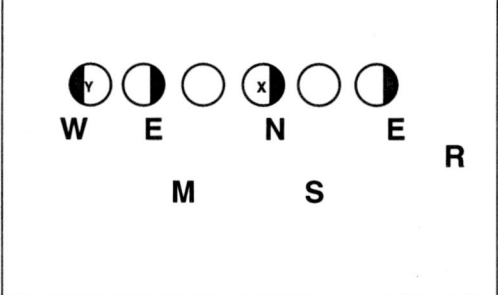

Figure 3-12. Okie walk

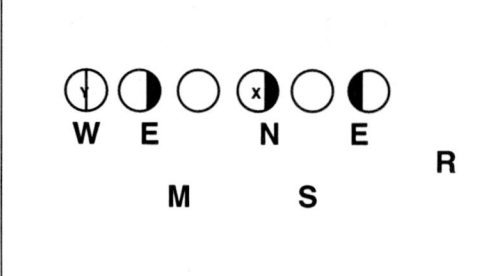

Figure 3-13. Okie inside

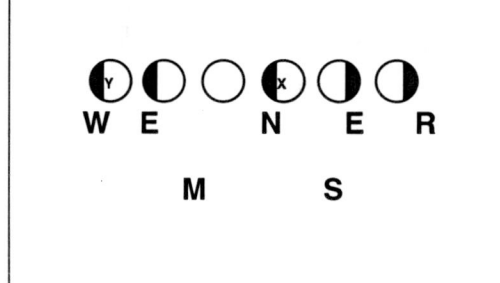

Figure 3-14. Eagle

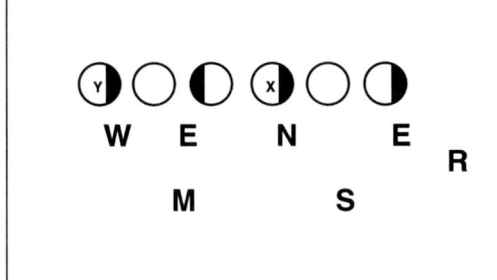

Figure 3-15. Strong eagle

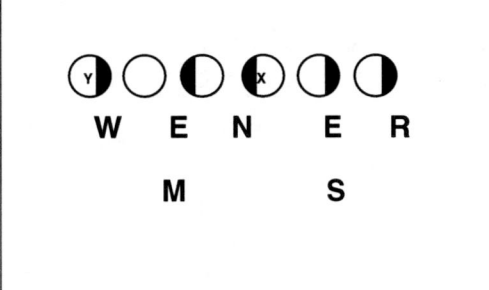

Figure 3-16. Double eagle

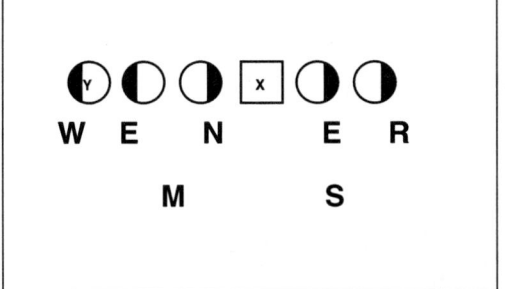

Figure 3-17. Split 5

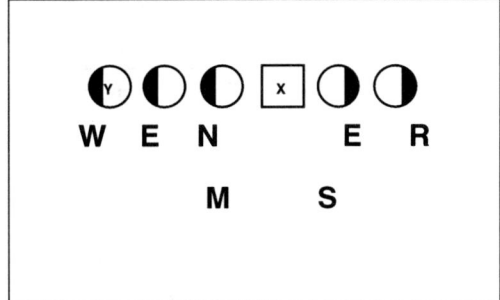

Figure 3-18. Split strong

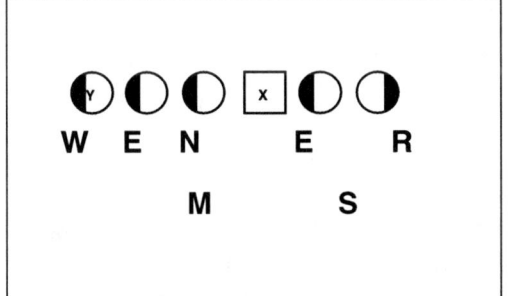

Figure 3-19. Split strong Tim

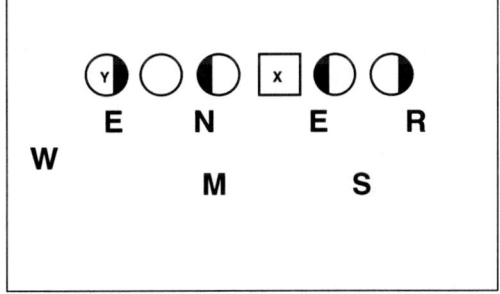

Figure 3-20. Tiger

Numbering System

Obviously, the use of even a few of these fronts would cause offenses recognition problems. However, the problem with multiple fronts is incorporating all those fronts without confusing your own players.

Most defensive coaches feel that it is best *not* to use rote memorization, but instead use a well-thought-out, systematic approach that allows players to build on prior knowledge and technique. This approach is best if you use a numbering system that gives players both alignment and technique. Coaches can use the numbering system in Figure 3-21 for shades or techniques. Coaches use this system as their guide. For example, an "over G" call places the tackles in a 32 alignment (Figure 3-22). An "under" call places the tackles in a 13 configuration (Figure 3-23). The tackle to the call has the first number and the tackle away from the call assumes the second number.

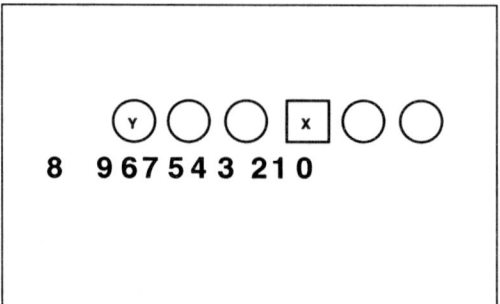

Figure 3-21. Numbering system

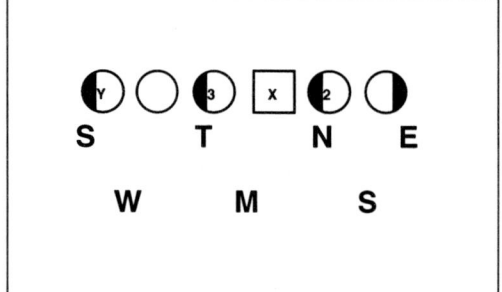

Figure 3-22. Over

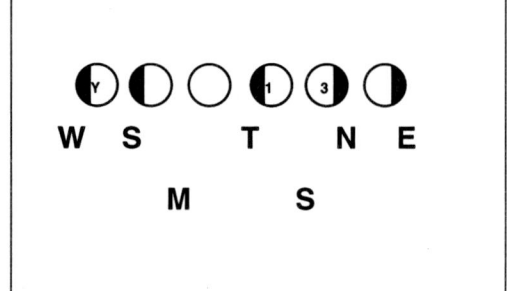

Figure 3-23. Under

Defensive ends get their alignments off the tackles' alignments. A 3-4 package (with a three down lineman look), can use two numbers for the ends, plus a word for the nose. In this package, the first word is for the nose followed by two numbers which affect the two ends. The first number aligns the strong end, with the second number controlling the weak end. Figures 3-24 and 3-25 are examples of this alignment protocol.

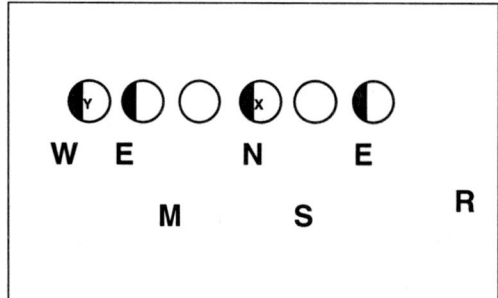

Figure 3-24. Strong 54

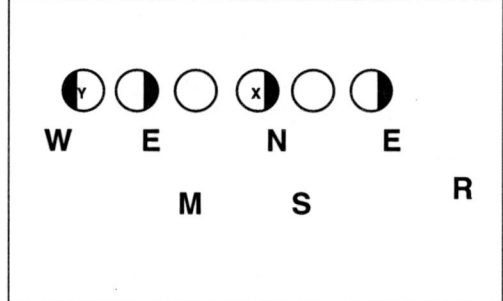

Figure 3-25. Weak 45

The following nose alignments are shown in Figure 3-26:
- Split (SPL) = 3 technique to the call
- Over strong (OS) = 2 technique to the call
- Strong (ST) = 1 technique to the call
- Weak (WK) = 1 technique away from the call
- Over weak (OW) = 2 technique away from the call
- Zip = 3 technique away from the call

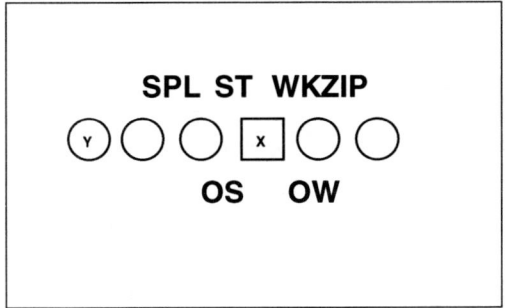

Figure 3-26. Nose alignments

As you have probably noticed, the vast majority of numbers are placed on the edges of offensive men. The only two head-up technique numbers in Figure 3-21 are for 0 technique and 6 technique. Some coaches will designate an inside shade on the guard as a 2i shade, and head-up as a 2 technique. An inside shade on the offensive tackle is a 4i shade and head-up on the tackle would be a 4 technique. Shades are divided into inside or outside shades. The outside shades are: 1, 3, 5, and 9 techniques. Inside shades are 2, 4, and 7 techniques.

Outside shades:
- 1 technique = Shade on center (If to the call, the defender will be in a +1 shade. If the shade is away from the strength call, he is referred to as a -1 shade.)
- 3 technique = Defender's inside foot splits the guard's crotch.
- 5 technique = Defender's inside foot splits the tackle's crotch.
- 9 technique = Defender's inside foot splits the end's crotch.

Inside shades:
- 2 technique = Defender's outside foot splits the guard's crotch.
- 4 technique = Defender's outside foot splits the tackle's crotch.
- 7 technique = Defender's outside foot splits the end's crotch.

Popular Fronts

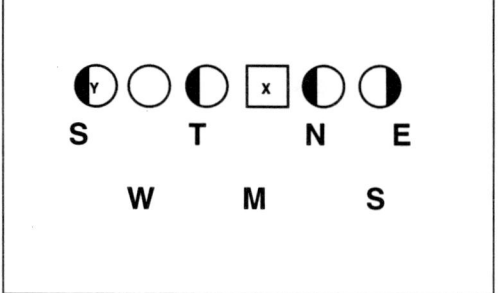

Figure 3-27. Over G (32)

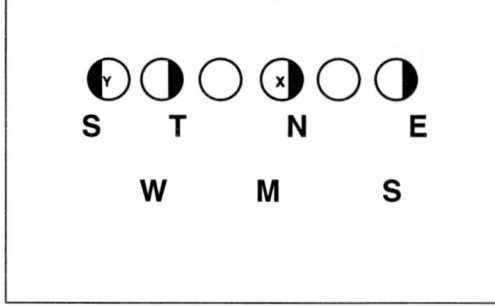

Figure 3-28. Wide (41)

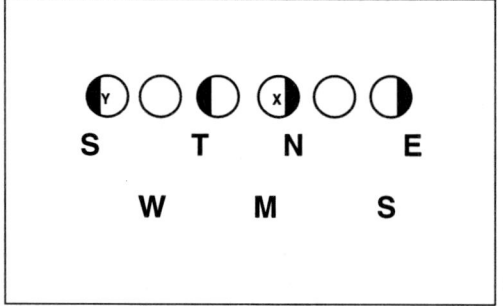

Figure 3-29. Over (31)

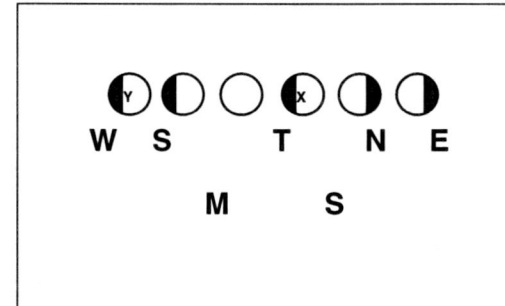

Figure 3-30. Under (13)

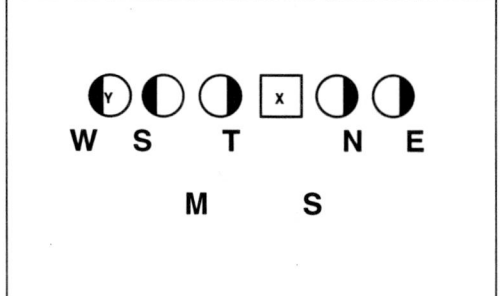

Figure 3-31. Under G (23)

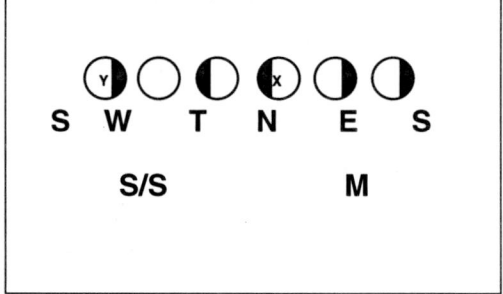

Figure 3-32. Bears (Strong 33)

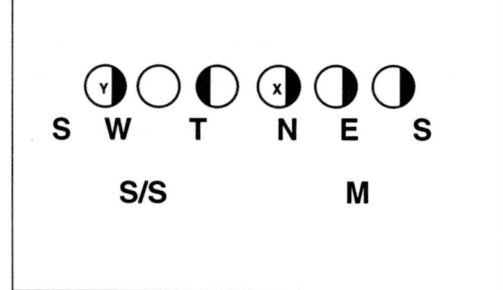

Figure 3-33. Weak Bears (Weak 33)

As a base rule, alignments are foot-to-crotch. However, there are nuances to each shade assignment.

Assigned shades are not set in concrete. They can change to meet the tactical situation. One nuance is a "loose" call. This tag places the defender foot-to-foot on the offensive lineman instead of foot-to-crotch. For example, a "loose" 3 technique has the defender placing his inside foot on the offensive lineman's outside foot, instead of his crotch. A "loose" 4 technique would place the defender's outside foot on the blocker's inside foot.

Another refinement on thickness of shade occurs when a defender notices a wide split by his alignment assignment. For example, if the 3 technique recognizes a wider than normal split by the guard, he will tighten down—or thicken—his alignment on the guard in anticipation of a down block on a trap, or midline play.

Should the guard take an abnormal split, the defender can make a "sink" call and move to a 2 technique. The "sink" call alerts linebackers that the defensive tackle will assume A gap responsibility, which in turn makes the onside linebacker a B gap player.

Another refinement is a "gap" call. This call places defenders in the gap according to the defender's respective alignment assignment. From there, the defender executes a hard upfield charge looking for penetration. For example, an "under gap" call would result in the defense illustrated in Figure 3-34.

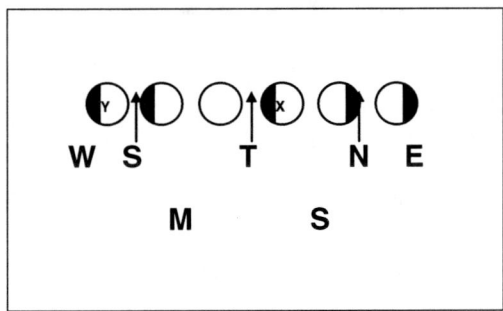

Figure 3-34. Under gap

Gaps

In addition to numbering shades, label gaps using letters (Figure 3-35). Gaps are assigned for every defensive front. Gap designation assigns gap, option, force/fill, cutback, and pass rush responsibilities.

Linemen should understand that their alignment assigns them gap responsibility. For example, a 3 technique is responsible for B gap. A 5 technique is charged with defending C gap.

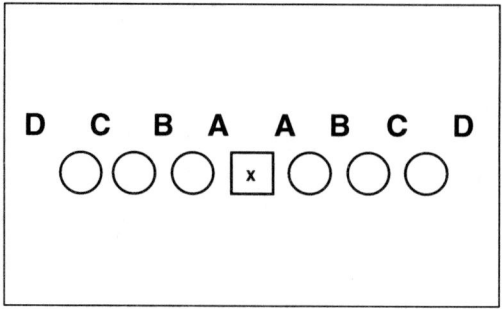

Figure 3-35. Gap designations

Defenders should also understand their gap may expand, contract, or change, according to the offensive block scheme. A reach block on a 3 technique serves to widen B gap, while a down block by the offensive tackle will cause a 5 technique to close and take B gap with a linebacker scraping to C gap.

In essence, the blocking scheme causes the 5 technique and an inside linebacker to exchange gap responsibilities. Gap definition can be expanded to distinguish between gaps to the strength call and away from the strength by tagging strongside gaps with a plus (+) designation. Weakside gaps can be tagged with a minus symbol (-). For example, strongside A is referred to as A+ while weakside A is considered A-.

Huddle/Player Designations

Just as you should be concerned with alignments at the line of scrimmage, when the offense breaks the huddle, you should be equally focused on where and how players huddle. You must coach up your players on pre-alignment also.

There are as many defensive huddle protocols as there are coaches. Some teams prefer huddles that are very formal with hand holds and the whole nine yards. Other coaches favor a more relaxed or informal structure. Various teams stagger personnel to better facilitate flip-flopping players.

Some coaches involve their defensive backs in the huddle, while other coaches prefer their defensive backs to be out of the huddle scanning the sideline areas for substitutions, or trick plays. The huddle used is entirely up to the individual coach and his needs.

Many coaches use a hanging huddle format. They feel this informal—yet efficient—structure allows them to better play no-huddle or up-tempo offenses. Some coaches feel teams which operate a formal huddle system can be forced out of their comfort zone when teams quick-huddle or go no-huddle. They also feel they spend too much practice time perfecting the formal huddle.

Figure 3-36 illustrates a hanging huddle. In the illustration, you can see the defense has a right and left end along with a right and left tackle. It is advantageous, however, to distinguish the ends and tackles (if you aren't flip-flopping) after the strength has been declared.

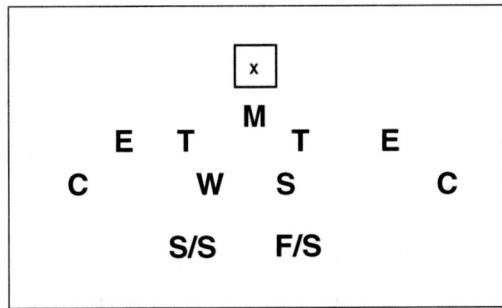

Figure 3-36. Hanging huddle

In this system, the defensive end to the call is *Stud*. The end away from the call is the *end*. The defensive tackle to the call is tagged as the *tackle*. The tackle away from the call is referred to as the *nose*. This nomenclature is helpful in many aspects of defensive line play (stunt game, for example).

In games where personnel is flip-flopped to take advantage of perceived mismatches—or to hide mismatches—some coaches stagger the affected linemen. For example, if they want to flip-flop the ends, they place the end that will go to the call (Stud) closer to the line of scrimmage than the end that will go weak.

The call end, Stud, has the right of way (Figure 3-37). The weak end will yield to Stud. This arrangement serves to facilitate a smooth transition should they have to cross paths going to their assigned alignments. The tackle has the right of way over the nose (Figure 3-38). Figures 3-39 and 3-40 show a total line flip-flop. In this scenario, the strong side—Stud and tackle—have the right of way.

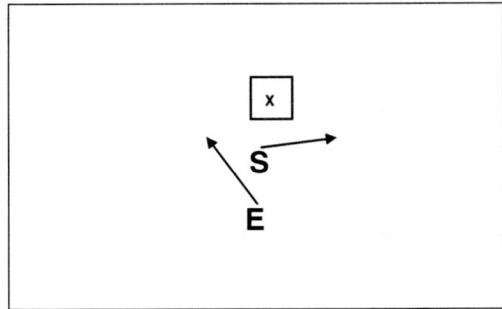

Figure 3-37. Stud has right of way

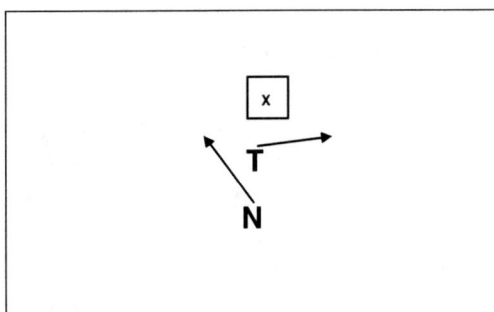

Figure 3-38. Tackle has right of way

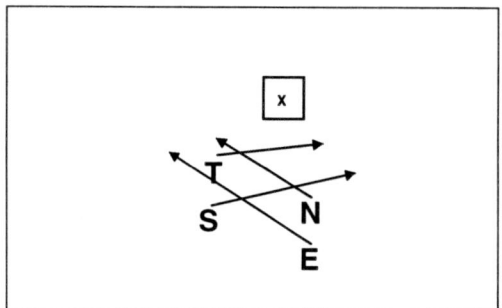

Figure 3-39. Total line flip-flop (right call)

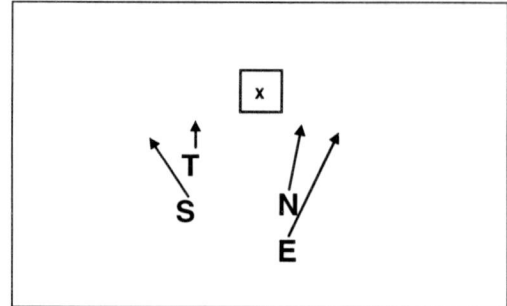

Figure 3-40. Total line flip-flop (left call)

Defensive Linemen's
Huddle/Pre-Snap Responsibilities

- Align properly in the hanging huddle.
- Listen intently for the defensive call.
- Align properly after the huddle.
- Listen for strength declaration and get aligned in the proper defense quickly. (Mike will make a "right" call for strong right and "left" for strong left. However, linemen should watch the offense leave the huddle and pick out the strength of the formation. It is everyone's responsibility to recognize and know the strength.)
- Listen for the linebackers to call out the backfield set. (Examples: I, split, weak, ace.) This call should offer tip-offs to the defensive linemen as to potential plays (scouting report).
- Listen for any checks, or alerts, from linebackers.
- Recognize pre-snap tip-offs (Examples: line splits, stances, eyes).
- Set up in a good stance, with proper weight distribution.
- Focus on the assigned key.

Basic Rulebook Rules Relevant to Defensive Line

- Defensive linemen should line up on the ball, not the offensive linemen. (They should take as much of the line of scrimmage as possible.)
- NFHS rules defenders are not allowed to cross the line of scrimmage at any time. (NCAA rules defenders can get back if they jump, as long as they don't make contact with an offensive man.)
- If an offensive man jumps, the defender may make instantaneous contact. However, if the defender strikes him late, it could result in offsetting penalties.
- Once an offensive lineman (from tackle to tackle) places his hand on the ground, he cannot pick it up off the ground. However, he may shift from a two-point stance

to a three- or four-point stance. (A skill player—receiver, back, tight end—can pick his hand up off the ground.)

- The ball should be recovered on all incomplete passes that don't cross the line of scrimmage. (Players should make the official blow the whistle to stop the play.)
- Any fumble may be advanced.
- There is no pass interference behind the line of scrimmage. All eligible receivers should be treated roughly. (However, holding can be called.)
- Defensive players may use unlocked hands, hand, or arm to ward off an opponent who is attempting to block them. However, the hand must be in advance of the elbow and contact must be at the shoulder level or below unless an opponent squats, ducks, or submarines.
- Defenders may push, pull, or ward off an opponent in an attempt to get to the runner or a loose ball.
- Offensive players simulating possession of the ball may be contacted. (However, this rule does not cancel the responsibility of any defensive player to exercise reasonable caution in avoiding any unnecessary contact.)
- Defenders may be clipped or blocked in the back if the blocker aligned on the line of scrimmage and was inside the free-blocking zone—which is a rectangular area extending four yards on either side of the snap and three yards behind each side of the line of scrimmage. (However, this rule doesn't apply after the ball has left the zone.)
- The snapper may lift the ball for lateral rotation but may not rotate end-for-end or change the location of the ball. (If the snapper places both hands on the ball, he may not remove one prior to the snap.)

4

Fundamentals

Fundamental is defined as "basic, essential, of central importance." This chapter will explore the techniques, or fundamentals, which are of central importance to effective defensive line play.

Included in this chapter are the building blocks of effective defensive line play. They include:

- Stance
- Alignment
- Key
- Takeoff
- Contact
- Separation
- Escape
- Pursuit
- Tackling
- Turnovers

Stance

Effective defensive line play hinges on an effective and functional stance. A faulty stance will doom a lineman from the start. Since he is on the line of scrimmage, things happen suddenly. A poor start will result in failure.

Most teams use five major stances. The first stance is the basic attack-read stance. The second stance is a "cobra" or sprinter's stance, which is utilized for pass rush. The third is a four-point stance, which may be used for a tough, or submarine, charge on the goal line. The other two stances involve a gap charge and a stance that facilitates quick movement on a called stunt.

Coaches should understand that you can't teach one stance for everyone. Line coaches should seek to tailor stances for each individual player to accommodate his unique physical characteristics.

A stance should be crafted which will allow the player to uncoil with maximum explosion, and quick movement. Even though stances will vary, some elements of the stance should be standard. The down hand should be placed four to six inches in front of the defender's helmet with 60 percent of the weight placed on the fingertips. The down hand should be in front of the big toe. The lineman should have 40 percent of his weight on his feet. The feet should have a toe to heel relationship with toes pointed straight ahead. The shaded foot should be back with the same-side hand down. The toes should be pointed slightly inside with knees and shoulders pointed straight ahead. There should be a Z in the knee. Feet should also be slightly wider than shoulder width with the heels pointed slightly outward. The heels must not be too high off the ground, especially the back foot. The uncovered, or free, hand (gap-side hand) should be cocked and held close to the ground. The tail should be slightly higher than the head. The defensive lineman's neck should be bulled with eyes looking straight ahead while seeing the ball in his peripheral vision.

In the cobra or jet package, linemen shift into a total pass rush mode. Linemen should think pass, and react to run. The defensive linemen should have 80 percent of their weight on the down hand. Coach him to really jack his tail up with less Z in the knee.

Linemen should focus more on the ball in the cobra stance. Feet are closer together and the stance is more elongated with the down hand more out in front of the head. The defensive lineman looks like a sprinter in the blocks.

Use the submarine, or tough, charge mainly in goal line situations. It can also be used in short yardage situations.

This stance is a low four-point stance with 90 percent of the weight on the hands with the hips higher than the head. The body is coiled, ready to penetrate low across the line of scrimmage, in an attempt to create a new line of scrimmage on the offensive side of the ball. The gap stance is very similar to the cobra stance in that it is more elongated than the basic read stance. There is less balance because there is little, if any, side-to-side movement.

The emphasis is on an upfield penetrating type of move. This type of stance better facilitates penetration than a stance used in a shade assignment.

The fifth stance to use is a move—or stunt—stance. This stance looks like the basic style of stance except 60 percent of weight is on the feet with the majority of the weight on the foot opposite the first step. For example, if a defender is making a hard inside move he should have most of his weight on the outside foot.

You may decide to manipulate the angle of a defensive lineman's stance. For example, versus option teams you can slightly cock your end's stance. This tilt better facilitates the end's ability to take the dive on the option as this stance automatically squeezes the off-tackle hole.

Alignment

Use the "credit card" rule on alignment. The defender wants to be the width of a credit card from being offside. He should align as close to the line of scrimmage as possible, right on the tip of the ball. If the center tips the ball upward, the defender should crowd even more. Care must be taken that the defender doesn't align on the opponent, but lines up on the tip of the ball.

Key

The defensive lineman should key the helmet of the offensive man he's aligned on. More specifically, he should key on the screw on the offensive player's helmet to the shade side. Again, the defensive lineman should also keep the ball in his peripheral vision.

In practice use a football painted green. The green ball blends in with the green grass which makes it harder to see peripherally. When a defender gets into the game with the brown ball on green grass, the ball really stands out. In passing situations, or in the cobra, gap, or tough packages, key the tip of the football.

Takeoff

Once the defensive lineman settles into his stance, he is ready to explode out on movement. On any offensive movement, he should immediately create a new line of scrimmage. Sound scouting will reveal what on offense moves first. It may be the quarterback's hands, foot, or butt.

Linemen should be conditioned to react to movement. Defensive drills should be initiated on ball movement, not on sound to condition defensive linemen to block out sound and react only to movement. Allow no gifts! Coaches can accept no excuses for mental errors on the cadence. However, be careful that linemen aren't intimidated into being late off the ball.

Defenders should visualize a string tied to the tip of the ball and the defensive lineman's nose. Defenders want their hands moving when the ball moves. Attacking blockers quickly eliminates or reduces the effectiveness of many blocks.

A defender should fall out of his stance leading with his hands, nose, and face while keeping his numbers over his toes. Defenders should come out of their hips but not lunge.

Linemen should take a power step, which is a six to eight inch step with the shaded foot. This is a short, controlled step. The first step should be quick and short. Linemen should get the foot back on the ground as quickly as possible. This allows the defensive lineman to facilitate a good base, or redirect, quickly. Care must be taken not to overstride and become off-balanced. The only benefit of a big first step is on pass plays.

Overstriding only serves to put a defensive lineman at a disadvantage because he is overextended and cannot react adequately to other blocks. A big first step doesn't allow defensive linemen to close on down blocks, for example. The power step should be followed with the second step, or base step. This base step results in the defender being in a near parallel stance.

Gap Takeoff

Most takeoff techniques involve a defensive player contacting an offensive player. However, defensive linemen using a gap technique seek to avoid contact and instead try to penetrate a gap between offensive linemen.

The defensive lineman will alter his stance from a balanced and solid base type stance to an elongated pass rush style. This stance facilitates an upfield thrust on offensive movement. Most linemen will use a swim, or slap, technique. Defensive linemen who use this charge seek to grab the offensive lineman, and use the offensive player's body to pull himself through the gap. The hand he uses depends upon his shade. The offhand and arm can be maneuvered through the gap using either a swim, or rip move.

Regardless of which move the defender uses, the key is to stay low. The danger of a swim move is the defensive man may come out of his stance too high.

Takeoff Maxims

- Quickness off the ball is an *attitude*.
- See the ball out of the corner of the eye (peripheral vision).
- First step is critical. (Foot replaces the hand. The step must be straight ahead.)
- Beat the opponent to the punch. (Get feet into the neutral zone.)
- Attack upfield two steps. (Get feet in the neutral zone. Create a new line of scrimmage.)
- Read on the run.
- Use good arm action.

- Lead with the hands.
- Stay low. (Don't raise up. Work at the same pad level as stance.)
- React to movement (ball/man), not sound.
- Vary voice inflection in get-off drills.
- Always go on movement in practice.

Takeoff Tips for Defensive Linemen

- Get pre-snap cues by looking at the offensive lineman's eyes (i.e., is he looking at a linebacker or a body part of yours?).
- Focus eyes on the screw on the offensive lineman's helmet.

Contact

Most coaches teach two types of contact techniques. Some coaches prefer hands only while others prefer a forearm/shoulder lift. Some coaches teach both. This section will include both techniques.

The late Fritz Shurmur, one of the greatest defensive coordinators in the history of the NFL, said that the use of hands was the number one technique a defensive lineman must master and that the ability to teach effective use of hands was the number one quality a defensive line coach should possess. The ability of a defender to neutralize the block of an offensive man in such a manner that the defensive lineman defeats the block, or gains an advantageous position over the blocker, is the goal of contact fundamentals.

Hand Shiver

The hand shiver is good for the majority of blocks (especially lateral-type blocks such as cutoff, reach, and cut, or when the defender is physically superior to the blocker). Coaches should use some hand drills with no feet involved when teaching the hand shiver technique.

The defender should lead with his eyes and hands. The hands are the fastest part of the body. The defender should keep his head and eyes up. The proper pad level is with the head below the opponent's face mask and in the V of the neck. He should roll his hips for added power.

The defender should strive to get the blocker on his heels. He should patter his feet on contact and stay square to the line of scrimmage. Thumbs should be pointed up to 12 o'clock with elbows rolled inside. When the thumb is at 12 o'clock, the elbow will be in.

The heel of the hand should be used to strike the opponent. The shaded hand (trail hand) should be placed on the near number of the offensive lineman and the gap hand (power hand) should grab cloth on the blocker's outside shoulder area (pec and cuff). The defender's back should be at a 45-degree angle. Straight-up movement should be avoided.

Coaching Points for Hand Shiver

- The defensive lineman should strike with the hard part of the hands. (i.e., heel and palm of hands)
- The defensive lineman should not wind up. (The strength of the blow comes from the quickness of the blow. All movement should be forward.)
- On contact, the defensive lineman should straighten out the arms. (Locking the arms out causes the large muscles of the back to be involved.)
- The defensive lineman should not bend his arms during the lockout. (A bent-arm lockout uses only the arm muscles (biceps-triceps), thereby minimizing the strength of the lockout.)
- The defensive lineman should attack with the hands, and then bring the feet. (If defenders try to strike and step at the same time, it will make the hands too slow.)
- On contact, the defensive lineman should simultaneously thrust the hips by flexing at ankles, knees, and hips to involve the large muscles of the lower body.
- Defenders who use hand shivers are harder to hold. (At the very least, holding will be more noticeable.)

Forearm/Shoulder Lift

A forearm shiver occurs when a defender drives his shoulder under the blocker's shoulder pad area, and into the blocker's chest. The defender follows up with an explosive hip roll, and an extension to a hand shiver, which creates separation.

As with a pure hand shiver, the blow should be followed up immediately with a foot buzz at the stalemate point. For the most part, the mechanics of the forearm/shoulder lift are not dissimilar to the hand shiver. Body position, leverage, and foot movements are congruent for both. The major difference is that the blow is struck with the back of the hand and top of the forearm. The offhand is still used to grasp the cuff area of the blocker.

Coaching Points for Forearm/Shoulder Lift

- Good for inside shades (i.e., 2-4-7 techniques)
- More powerful than hand shiver
- Good for undersized defenders

- Effective against straight-on blockers
- More forceful versus blockers which have a running start at the defender

Contact Maxims

- Pads out
- Contact with eyes, shoulder pads and elbows locked
- Strike with hard part of hands
- Don't give up chest
- Strike with top of pads
- Play from the ground up
- Footwork
- Body control
- Thumbs up, squeeze elbows
- Eyes low then rise (Lead with helmet and eyes.)

Separation

Gaining separation is crucial to the defensive lineman's ability to make plays. This is where the kinship between wrestling and defensive line play manifests itself.

It doesn't matter if the defensive lineman has a million dollar stance and takeoff if he cannot defeat the block, gain separation, and get into the proper pursuit angle. Without effective separation, the defender cannot progress into the next phase—escape.

An adequate stance and takeoff will serve to give the defender an advantage by getting the blocker on his heels. Part of the separation process involves the large muscles of the upper and lower body. Correct angles at the ankles, knees, and hips add to the effect. Players who play pad-under-pad tend to have better leverage. Leverage helps keep defenders from being held. Holding is harder—or at least more noticeable—if the defender's arms are fully extended.

Separation Maxims

- Gain lock out
- Feet can't stop
- Low man wins (leverage and separation)
- Fight pressure, don't run around blocks
- Throw off the block, get clean, never stay blocked

Escape

After the defensive lineman defeats the block and separates, he must escape the blocker and get into the correct pursuit angle. Defenders must understand that they should not try to escape until they *control* the blocker. Escape attempts before the block is controlled can result in the defender being pancaked.

Most coaches teach several escape moves. The use of these moves depends upon the point of attack and the blocker/defender relationship.

Rip

If the ball is in the immediate area, the defensive lineman can use a rip to escape. The defensive lineman must understand that in order to execute the rip, he must have a pad-under-pad relationship to the blocker. He also must understand that as he comes off the rip, the ball will be in the immediate vicinity.

Crossface Wipe

If the ball is two or more gaps away, the defender can use a crossface wipe. This technique involves pulling down the blocker's playside shoulder and swimming—or the "wax off" of *Karate Kid* fame. The defender should keep his shoulders square to the line of scrimmage if the ball is in position to cut back.

Snatch

The snatch move is used when defenders are far removed from the point of attack. The defender—after he locks his arms out—will grab the blocker and throw him opposite the direction the defender wants to go. The defender may need to drop step or give ground as he executes this maneuver.

The snatch and throw will serve to gain separation, as well as propel the defender toward the ball. The defender finishes the escape move by stepping and driving for the ball.

Backdoor

The backdoor escape maneuver is used when the defense is beaten, or when the blocker over-commits to the playside. In this case, the defender escapes *inside* the blocker and runs tight to the blockers' heels to the ball.

Spin

The spin escape move should be used only as a last resort. It is used only when the defense is pinned inside the point of attack and the ball has passed the cutback point.

The defender will pivot off his outside foot, and lean into the blocker while throwing his backside shoulder and elbow in the desired direction.

A key coaching point is to keep the shoulders down and spin tight to the blocker. This move is very similar to the discus throw pass rush move illustrated in the pass rush section of this book.

Steer

The steer technique is used when the ball is in an adjacent, inside gap. The defensive lineman must maintain a posture that allows him to defend his assigned gap while squeezing, or compressing, the blocker into the adjacent hole in an attempt to constrict, or squeeze the hole. The defender must anticipate a bounce-out and keep his outside shoulder free.

Compress Technique

The compress technique is used in the following situations: after the ball reaches a point of no return; when a blocker needs to be squeezed away from a defender's gap responsibility; or when the defender has a disadvantaged fit on a blocker (e.g., the blocker has his head between the defender and the ballcarrier) and the pursuer has to crossface to get to the ball or regain his gap responsibility to pursue the ball. The concept of defeating blockers while getting to the ball and helping close inside running seams should be stressed.

Inside Shade Player (with proper gap control)

- *If the ball comes to an inside shade player and stays inside the tackle box but outside his gap responsibility, and there is a threat of a cutback,* the lineman should steer the blocker and constrict/squeeze the running seam by pushing the blocker's outside pec up, and pull his inside arm to turn the blocker's shoulders to the sideline. The defender should squeeze the next gap outside and be ready for a cutback. He should twist his tail into the hole.
- *If the ball comes to the defender and goes outside the tackle box and there is no threat of cutback,* he should steer the blocker by pushing his outside pec up, and pull his inside arm to turn his shoulders to the sideline. After turning the shoulders, the defender can give ground and rip, swim, or crossface wipe as he steps across the blocker's face and pursues the ball.
- *If the ball goes away from the defensive lineman and stays in the tackle box and there is a threat of cutback, or if the ball goes outside the tackle box,* the lineman should steer the blocker by pushing his outside pec, and pull his inside arm to turn his shoulders to the sideline. He should then power rip under, squeeze to the ball flat on the line of scrimmage, or trail deep if he is a contain player.

Outside Shade Player (with proper gap control)

- *If the ball comes to an outside shade player and stays inside the tackle box and inside of his gap responsibility,* he should steer the blocker inside to constrict the running seam, and try to make the ball bounce outside. The defender should steer by pushing the blocker's inside pec up, and pull his outside arm to turn his shoulders to the inside. He should constrict the inside running seam.
- *If the ball comes to the defender and goes outside the tackle box,* he should steer the blocker by pushing his inside pec up, and pull his outside shoulder to turn his shoulders inside. The defender then should power rip, or crossface wipe, come off the block, and make the play.
- *If the ball goes away from the defensive lineman and stays in the tackle box, and there is a threat of cutback, or if the ball goes outside the tackle box,* the lineman should steer and squeeze the blocker by pushing his inside pec up, and pull his outside arm to turn his shoulders to the inside. If the ball stays in the tackle box, he should squeeze/constrict the cutoff.
- *If the defender is a squeeze player and the ball bounces outside the tackle box,* he should drop step, power rip, swim, or wipe, and pursue flat down the line of scrimmage. If he is a contain player, he should trail and look for BCR (bootleg, counter, reverse).

Disadvantaged Inside (Hooked or Reached as an Outside Shoulder Player)

The defender should steer the blocker by pushing his outside pec up, and pulling his inside arm to turn his shoulders to the sideline. He should use his head to drive through the V of the blocker's neck. He should then drop step, and power rip, swim, or wipe across the blocker's face and pursue the ball.

Escape Maxims

- Don't stay blocked; escape and go.
- Gap hand is the power hand (push).
- Covered hand is the trail hand (pull).
- Control the blocker.
- Rip when ball is in the area.
- Crossface wipe when ball is wider. (Playside arm jerks down, the swim is by the backside arm.)
- Snatch when ball is very wide.

Pursuit

Once the defender has separated and escaped, he moves into the pursuit phase of the play. Pursuit, first and foremost, is a *mental* task. It is an all-out effort of running to the ball with proper angles.

Defensive linemen must have the desire to get to the football. Defenders must shed the block; if blocked, don't stay blocked; if knocked to the ground, get up! The ground is a hot stove!

Effective pursuit breaks the opponent's will to win by showing a fanatical desire to get to the ball. Pursuit facilitates gang tackling. Gang tackling affects runners and helps create turnovers.

Pursuit also serves to eliminate big plays, and helps to cover up mistakes. Defensive linemen must take individual, as well as group, pride in pursuit. It has been said that a man's value can be measured by his distance from the football when the whistle blows. Dynamic pursuit must be expected and ingrained in defensive line personnel.

Defensive coaches must demand, and drill, sound pursuit techniques. You can choose to grade pursuit when you break down game films. Grade each player using the following 6 elements of hustle:

Elements of Hustle

- Changing speed
- Turning and bursting to the ball versus passes (three-step change of direction)
- Not being passed by another positional player
- Getting off the ground
- Making the hit
- Getting in the picture

Elements of Loaf

- Not changing speed
- Not turning and bursting to the ball versus passes (three-step change of direction)
- Getting passed by another positional player
- Staying on the ground
- Turning down a hit
- Not getting in the picture

Loafs may be graded after each game, selected scrimmages, or unit work. If a player falls into any of the six elements of a loaf, the defensive team can run a designed hustle course one time per loaf. The hustle course concept was borrowed from Allen Mogridge, assistant coach at the University of North Carolina.

Pursuit Angles

In addition to fostering pride in pursuit, the defensive line coach must coach proper pursuit angles. Attitude and correct angles are the two most important elements of pursuit. Defenders must first play good technique and execute their base responsibility, then take a good angle to the ball. Figures 4-1 and 4-2 show pursuit angles on wide plays, strong and weak.

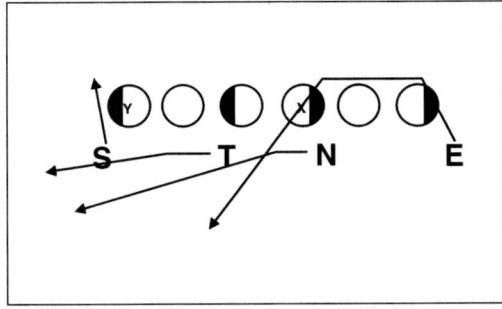

Figure 4-1. Wide play strong

Wide Play Strong Assignments

S: Fills. Fits between end-of-line offensive blocker and defensive force man.
T: Leverage. Inside-out to the ball.
N: Quick chase. Looks for fumbled snap to cutback.
E: Chases. Looks for BCR (bootleg-counter-reverse) close to ball then run through the ball's initial spot.

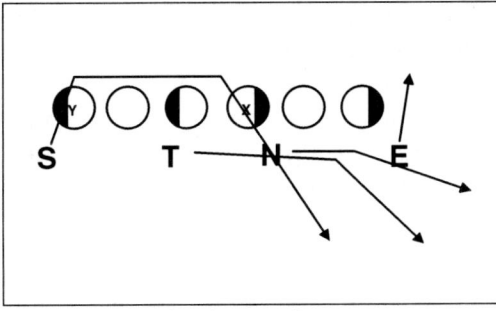

Figure 4-2. Wide play weak

Wide Play Weak Assignments

E: Fills.
N: Leverage.
T: Quick chase.
S: Chases.

Pursuit Benefits

- Creates renown as a *swarming* defense. (Swarming defenses make things happen.)
- Makes a good defensive unit a great defensive unit.
- Makes a defensive team a gang-tackling team.
- Minimizes long touchdowns.
- Covers up mistakes.
- Discourages opponents.
- Creates turnovers.

Pursuit Maxims

- Desire is the #1 requirement. There is always some way to get to the ballcarrier.
- Work through the blocker; fight pressure. Don't go around a blocker.
- Throw off the blocker. Get clean. Never stay blocked. Accelerate off the block. Avoid blockers on the way.
- Take an inside-out angle. Never follow the same colored jersey.
- Speed. Speed. Speed.

Tackling

The number one asset in tackling—as it is in pursuit—is desire. It is often said that tackling is 90 percent desire and 10 percent technique. Vince Lombardi has been quoted as saying that tackling is easier to teach than blocking, because tackling is more natural. He used the metaphor that, "If a man was running down the street with everything you own, you won't let him get away. That's tackling." Tacklers must approach tackling with the mindset that they must make the play. They should never assume that someone else will make the play.

Three Phases of Tacking

Approach

The single most important coaching point in the approach phase is to "come to balance." Defenders shouldn't be out of control when facing a one-on-one situation. Don't be out of control. However, don't break down either. A moving ballcarrier will always have the advantage over a tackler who is dead in the water.

"Come to balance" means the tackler should gather his momentum and drop his tail. He should close his power angles (arms and knees). Tacklers should close the distance early in the play, and keep their feet buzzing as they near the contact point. Tacklers should focus on the runner's belt buckle.

Contact

The ideal tackling fit is to have good knee bend, a flat back, head and eyes up, and arms wrapped, while grabbing cloth. Pop—at the point of contact—comes from the coordination of hip roll, thrusting the arms, and using the strongest parts of the body: the lower back and legs. The arms should be thrust—or shot upward—securing the ballcarrier by grabbing cloth.

Finish

The culmination of the play is dependent upon the combination of contact and leg drive. The finish is enhanced by a good base, and the rapid-fire movement of the tackler's feet.

The tackler should seek to knock the ballcarrier backwards and not allow him to fall forward. Leg drive serves to limit arm tackles or defenders reaching for the ballcarrier.

Tackling Situations

From the Side (Angle)

Contact should be on the near number with the head sliding across the bow. Placing the head across the bow will result in fewer arm tackles and supply more power to the tackle.

Care should be taken, however, that contact is made on the near number or the tackler may overshoot the target and lose leverage—or the angle, thereby allowing the ballcarrier to cut back. Tackling at ball level will cause the tackler to either have his head or shoulder pad on the ball, depending upon which arm the ball carrier has the ball in—this will facilitate more turnover possibilities.

Near the Boundary

Tacklers should attack the near shoulder by hitting through it and forcing the ballcarrier out of bounds. They should always use the boundary as an extra defender.

Open Field

Tacklers should close ground quickly and come to balance near the contact point. Defenders should know where their nearest help is and leverage the runner that way. Tacklers should avoid giving the ballcarrier a two-way go.

Head On

If the tackler is in a confined area—such as on or near the line of scrimmage—he should, if possible, place his face on the ball. This action allows the tackler to keep his head up, and see what he is hitting. And, ideally, it will result in fumbles.

Last Chance (Desperation)

In a last-ditch attempt to get the ballcarrier to the ground as he is speeding downfield past the defense, defenders may have to heel-slap or ankle-swipe the ballcarrier after diving as a last resort.

Tackling Dos and Don'ts

Tackling Dos

- Keep the head up. (Bull the neck.)
- See what you hit. (Keep eyes open.)
- Focus on the runner's belt buckle.
- Keep a good base. (Don't cross over.)
- Wrap up the ballcarrier.
- Hit through the ballcarrier. (Accelerate and widen feet on contact.)
- Hit on the rise.
- Tackle ball level. (This technique allows the tackler to get his face, with neck bulled, or shoulder on the ball, forcing more turnovers.)

Tackling Don'ts

- Do not lose vision of target.
- Do not stop feet at contact point.
- Do not use a narrow base.
- Do not lunge—or reach—for the ballcarrier.
- Do not forget to wrap up.

Turnovers

Turnovers are an immediate benefit of good tackling. When a defense tackles well fumbles occur. When defenders are taught to tackle at ball-level either the tackler's face or shoulder pad will be on the ball. The first man on the scene will ensure the tackle, while the second and all subsequent tacklers should club, pull, push, or punch the ball.

There are two strategies on how to treat a fumbled ball. Defenders can either *fall on the ball* or *scoop and run*. Variables, such as the score and time remaining, enter into this decision.

Fall on the Ball

If a defender is in a scrum situation with a lot of other bodies around, it would be best to simply fall on the ball. Defenders should also use the fall-on technique when their team is leading late in the game.

A fundamentally sound fall-on technique would require the defender to pull the ball to his middle while protecting the ball with arms, chest, and stomach. Defenders should take their top leg and pull the knee to the chest. The defender should try to turn his back to the nearest offensive player(s) while finishing in the fetal position.

A good coaching point is to have the defender secure the ball by covering the tips with his hands so the ball can't be leveraged out in a pile up. In many cases, the person who has the ball first in a pile doesn't end up with it after everyone unpiles.

Scoop and Run

The antithesis of the fall-on technique is a defender picking up the ball and running with it. This scoop and score mentality is best when a fumble occurs in the open field without a lot of traffic, or when the defense is behind late in the game. Also, blocked fourth down punts or field goal attempts should be scooped and run with.

The proper technique for a scoop and score scenario would involve the defender having good knee bend, scooping the ball with the hands *under* the ball, and keeping the ball side leg slightly back to avoid accidentally kicking it.

5

Block Reads and Reactions

This chapter will break down alignments into outside and inside shades. The chapter will also illustrate the various blocks used against these shades, and the desired defensive reactions to them.

Before getting to the individual alignments and the various types of blocks, the chapter will explore the most commonly used one-on-one, and combo, blocks that are universally used by offenses. These blocks will be explored in detail and defensive counter measures will be illustrated. Individual blocks will be broken down into inside and outside shades.

Individual Blocks/Reactions for Outside Shades

- Base
- Down/jump-through
- Reach
- Pass set

Base (Figure 5-1)

This is the number one block defensive linemen must defeat. The defender should keep his shoulders square to the line of scrimmage, steer the blocker inside, and constrict the running lane by pushing the blocker's inside pec and pulling his outside arm to turn the blocker's shoulders to the inside (refer to the steer technique section in Chapter 4).

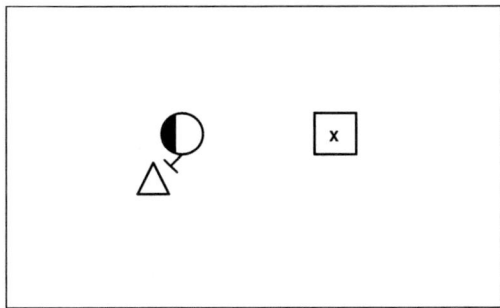

Figure 5-1. Base

Hand placement should be above the defender's own eyes. The defender must keep his outside arm and leg free for a bounce-out. If the defensive lineman feels no pressure, he must realize he is running around the block. When the ballcarrier commits, the defensive lineman must disengage and pursue.

Down/Jump-Through (Figure 5-2)

The defensive lineman should never run around the tail of a down block. Instead, he should get a piece of the blocker, and close through the blocker's hip.

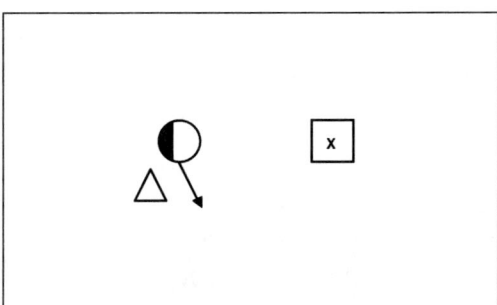

Figure 5-2. Down/jump-through

If the defender can get his offhand on the blocker, the ability to play a trap block—or take dive—is enhanced. The defensive lineman takes the first thing that shows off the down block. He will far shoulder or wrong arm any inside-out block.

If the blocking scheme is a jump-through, the defensive lineman should "collapse"— or work down the line of scrimmage looking for cutbacks. A jump-through usually involves a scoop or zone block by an adjoining offensive lineman. If the defensive lineman can get his outside hand engaged on the offensive lineman's hip, and—if possible—grab cloth, this would serve to propel the defensive lineman into the next gap and away from the scooper. This propulsion will also serve to speed the defender on a good pursuit angle and an advantageous position to better play the cutback. When the ball crosses the line of scrimmage the defensive lineman should take the correct pursuit angle.

Reach (Figure 5-3)

The total defensive scheme is in jeopardy if an outside shade is reached. The three basic types of reach blocks are:
- Tight reach
- Wide reach
- Arc reach

Figure 5-3. Reach

Tackles facing a reach block should try to get to a spot one yard outside the reach man, and two yards deep—the 2x1 rule. Ends facing a reach block should follow the 4x1 rule—four yards deep and one yard outside the offensive lineman.

Defensive linemen should take their eyes to their respective spot and find the ball when they get there; end up in the same outside shade alignment as they started; work to keep their outside shoulder free and work upfield at a 45-degree angle, and outside to the spot. They must not fly out because it would offer an inviting cutback lane.

Defenders should keep their feet back and use great extension. Defensive linemen should strive to keep their inside foot outside the blocker's outside foot with a long-arm/short-arm technique. The defender should push with his outside arm, and pull with his inside arm, at a 45-degree angle.

If the defender feels he is getting reached, he should throw his hips outside. The defender should never expose his chest, or allow the blocker to get his head outside and squared up. The defensive lineman should always keep his hips outside and in the hole.

Another key versus the reach block is to keep a low pad level, with hips behind the plane of the shoulders. Three major causes of getting reached are:

- Not locking out the arms
- Stepping inside on the snap
- False stepping on the snap

Pass Set (Figure 5-4)

As a base rule, the defender should rush through his assigned gap (rush lane). Inside defenders (tackles) should collapse the pocket. A three technique normally has a two way go (i.e., he can rush A or B gap versus a pass play). Outside defenders (ends) should force the quarterback to step up into the pocket.

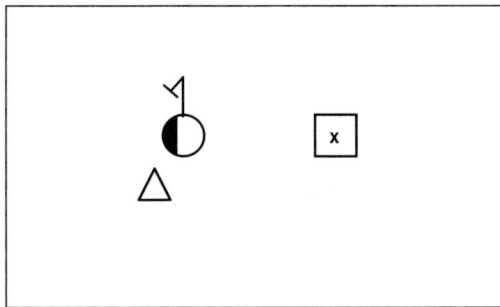

Figure 5-4. Pass set

The total scheme dictates whether the defensive linemen have the option of exchanging rush lanes. A "hot" call—where another defender is on an outside stunt—would allow the defensive lineman to go under a pass set. The outside defender now has cage (contain) on the quarterback. All defensive linemen in outside shades to the stunt side can go under pass sets.

Points of Emphasis for Outside Shades

- Stance
- Get-off
- Keys
- Eyes
- Hand and helmet placement
- Attack
- Gap control
- Lockout
- Separate

Outside Shade Maxims (1, 3, 5, 9 Techniques)

- Shoe-to-crotch tight on the ball (ability level)
- Three-point base stance with the inside foot back and shaded hand down
- Toe-to-heel stagger
- Six-inch power step from base
- Concentration on the screw on the front of the opponent's helmet
- Shaded hand = trail hand; gap or free hand = power hand

Basic Responsibilities for Outside Shades

- Protect gap responsibility.
- *Never* be reached.
- Close all down blocks (collapse). Protect the linebacker. Get hands on the blocker.
- Pursue all plays away (collapse). Squeeze flat to prevent cutbacks. No team wins without great effort backside. Once the ball crosses the line of scrimmage, take a deep angle to the ball.
- *Never* run around the tail of the blocker.
- *Never, ever* be passive. Attack at all costs.
- Rush passer through the prescribed rush lane.

Individual Blocks/Reactions For Inside Shades

- Base
- Shoeshine
- Outside release
- Pass

Base (Figure 5-5)

This is the number one block an inside shaded defender must defeat. The defensive lineman should keep his shoulders square to the line of scrimmage while steering the blocker outside and constricting the running lane. The inside shade defender should pull the blocker's inside cuff with his inside arm while pushing the pec area with his outside arm (steer technique). Hand placement should be above the defender's own eyes to ensure low pad level. The defensive lineman must keep his inside shoulder and leg free until the ball is no longer a cutback threat. If the defender feels no pressure, he is running around the block. He *must* hold the point. When the ballcarrier commits, the defender must disengage.

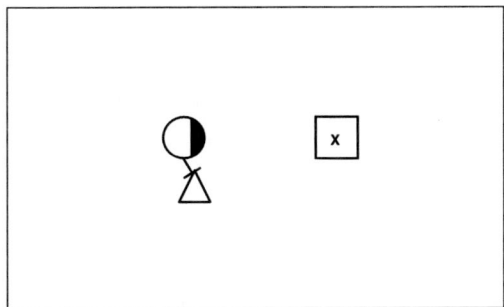

Figure 5-5. Base

Shoeshine (Figure 5-6)

This particular block occurs whenever an offensive lineman seeks to place himself between an inside shade defender and the point of attack. In Figure 5-6, the guard will try to get his right ear on the inside knee or thigh board of the inside technique. The key to defeating this block is to play it from the ground up.

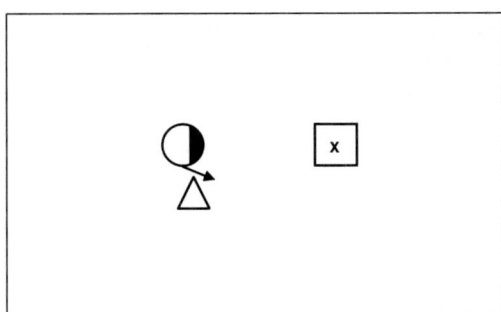

Figure 5-6. Shoeshine

The defender should make effective use of a hand shiver and keep his legs and hips back. The defensive lineman should flatten down the line of scrimmage with no penetration unless the ball is in the immediate area. The inside technique should think fumbled snap to cutback. Any time a 2 or 4 technique gets a shoeshine block, they should be alert for a fumbled snap. They have an excellent chance to recover any fumbled center-quarterback exchange. If there is no exchange problem, they flatten to play cutback.

Outside Release (Figure 5-7)

Defensive linemen should recognize an outside release on their first step. They should get their eyes inside immediately. The next lineman inside will be the key for trap, dive, or zone. On outside releases, tackles should think trap. Ends should think option/dive on outside releases. If a defender reads an inside-out block coming from the pull lane, he should attack and spill the ball. Some teams which play inside shades may have the inside shade defender read the next offensive lineman inside. In order to do this, you must have an exceptional player.

Figure 5-7. Outside release

Pass Set (Figure 5-8)

The defender should rush the passer in the prescribed rush lane. A defensive lineman should not allow an outside pass protector to block him one-on-one without a chip. An inside shade is in a direct line to the quarterback on a level 3 drop.

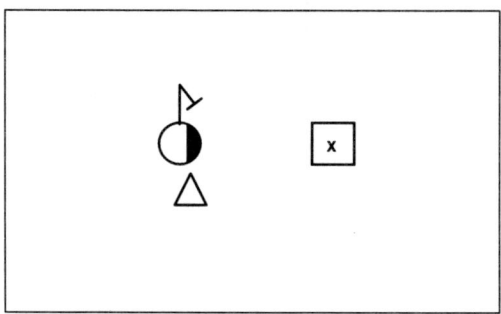

Figure 5-8. Pass set

Some teams choose to trap an inside shade off a pass set read. This puts the defender in conflict. Should he sell out on the rush, or will he have to slow his pass rush until he is certain it isn't an influence trap? That's a decision which must be made by the coaching staff. It is best to sell out on the rush unless your opponent has shown the propensity to trap off this action. If so, the defender will have to slow his rush and look to the next lineman inside to get a definite key. Most teams will usually give the guard at least a one hand assist from the center on pass plays. This should serve as a tip-off as to the play.

Points of Emphasis for Inside Shades

- Stance
- Get-off
- Keys
- Eyes
- Hand and helmet placement
- Attack
- Gap control
- Lockout
- Separate

Inside Shades Maxims (2, 4, 7 Techniques)

- Shoe-to-crotch tight on the ball (ability level)
- Three-point base stance with the outside foot back and shaded hand down
- Toe-to-heel stagger
- Six-inch power step from base
- Concentration on the screw on the front of the opponent's helmet
- Shaded hand = trail hand; gap or free hand = power hand

Basic Responsibilities for Inside Shades

- Protect gap responsibility.
- Keep inside leverage.
- *Never* get shoeshined (quick chase).
- Close if blocker doesn't block you.
- *Never* get scooped by next lineman inside.
- No team wins without great effort backside. (After defeating shoeshine, squeeze flat to prevent cutback lanes.)
- Rush in prescribed rush lane.

Combo Blocks

- Trap
- Scoop
- Zone
- Double-team
- Fold (inside/outside)

Trap (Figure 5-9)

The defender should squeeze, and replace the down blocker. The defensive lineman should try to get his outside hand on the offensive lineman's hip, or base of the numbers. The defensive lineman gets his eyes to the pull lane and spill any inside-out block. He will throw his outside shoulder at the inside thigh of the trapper.

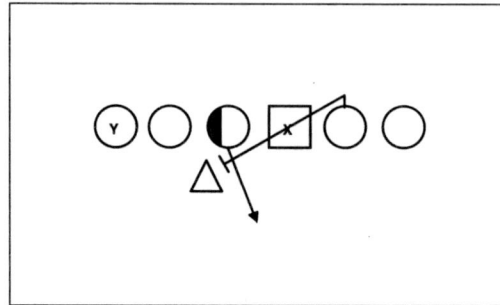

Figure 5-9. Trap

After contact the defender shouldn't sit on the line of scrimmage but should work slightly upfield to force the ballcarrier to run the hump. A common mistake most defenders make is to close too far and too flat. It is advisable to attack the trapper and square up in the hole. The defender should stay on his feet and reach with his inside arm to tackle the ballcarrier.

Scoop (Figure 5-10)

A scoop block may start out as a jump-through where the playside lineman seeks to avoid contact with the defensive lineman, or it may begin as a two-on-one block with the playside offensive lineman slipping to the next level.

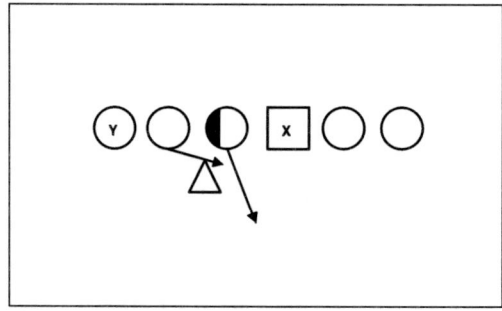

Figure 5-10. Scoop

Jump-Through Scoop (Figure 5-11)

The primary objective on the jump-through technique is to get the lead blocker on a level two defender quickly. The blocker will usually lead with a parallel step and a rip and dip motion with his backside arm. He is, in essence, avoiding a defender who might hold him up, or knock him off his course, to the inside defender. From all appearances, the jump-through looks like a down block, which could be followed with a trap block.

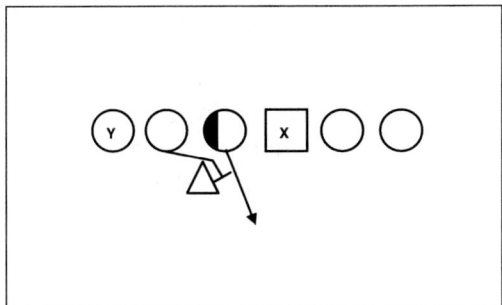

Figure 5-11. Jump-through scoop

Correct defensive technique will serve to play both a jump-through and a trap play. The defender should seek to replace the down block with his body. He should try to grab or strike the offensive man's closest hip area with his backside hand. The defender should grab cloth or shove the blocker with his outside hand. If he can grab cloth, this would serve to pull the defender toward the offensive man and away from the adjoining offensive man who is seeking to block him. The grab or shove should be followed up with the defender's outside leg snapping into a crossover move. This will make it harder for the outside blocker to cutoff the defender. At this point, the defender should take a good pursuit angle.

Two-on-One Scoop (Figure 5-12)

This tag team block is different from the jump-through scoop in that the lead blocker doesn't try to avoid the defender to be scooped. As a matter of fact, he seeks to block the defender until the backside blocker takes over.

This block may look like a base block or double-team early. The defender should play it like a base block and squeeze with shoulders square. This would serve to take

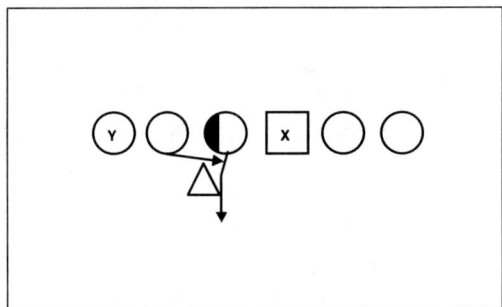

Figure 5-12. Two-on-one scoop

the defender away from the primary blocker. Unlike the base or double-team block, the defender will feel the setup man trying to slip off inside. The defender must not be driven off the line of scrimmage, or allow the inside man off inside on a linebacker. If the defender can grab the slip blocker with his playside hand it would serve to keep the blocker off the linebacker and keep the defensive lineman away from the second blocker.

The defensive lineman should stay low, and stay in the crease, keeping his playside (scoopside) shoulder and leg free. Punching or grabbing the scooper's hip area instead of his shoulder will keep the defender lower, and will expose less blocking surface. He should also twist his butt to the play, and keep his feet in the neutral zone. He should seek to get his feet to the next offensive lineman.

The defender should never allow the primary blocker to get his head across the defender's body. An observant defender can expect this type of block by observing line splits and on-the-line and the off-the-line offensive linemen. The alignment in Figure 5-13 should alert the 3 technique that a power scoop might be coming. After the defender defeats the power scoop, he should think cutback to a good pursuit angle.

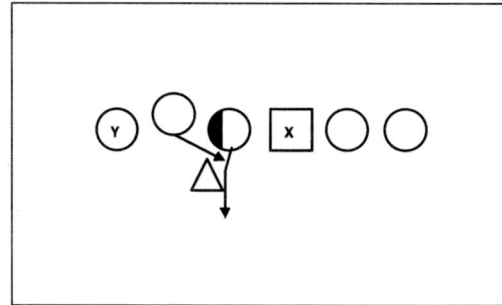

Figure 5-13. This alignment alerts the 3 technique that a power scoop might be coming.

Zone (Figure 5-14)

Defensive linemen should treat the zone scheme as a reach block. Defenders, upon recognizing the zone scheme, should attack and press upfield while extending their arms to deepen the blockers. Defenders should keep their shoulders square to the line of scrimmage, which helps defeat cutbacks. Defenders should understand that gaps move. Gaps can widen—or shrink—depending upon the blocking scheme. Zone schemes stretch defenders' gaps.

The zone scheme serves to move and widen gap responsibilities as the play develops. As the ball moves laterally, defenders must react by leveraging their gap responsibility as the play develops. Again, it is important for defenders to attack or pressure the line of scrimmage. This upfield pressure serves to reduce the angles and

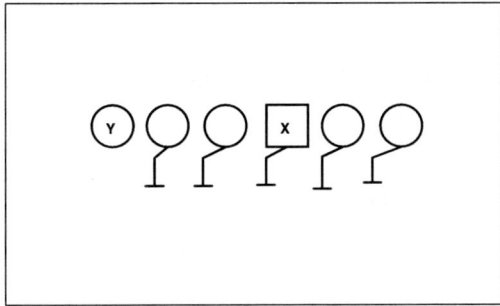

Figure 5-14. Zone

options for the offense, and make gaps smaller. Flat, lateral angles instead of vertical angles only invite cutbacks.

Double-Team (Figure 5-15)

The double-team is played just like a reach block. The post blocker will seek to leverage the defender's playside number or sternum area, while the drive man seeks to drive the defensive lineman off the ball. The only major difference between the defender's reaction to the double-team or reach block, is an exaggerated hip swivel when playing the double-team. Just as in a reach block the position of the hip is more important than that of the head.

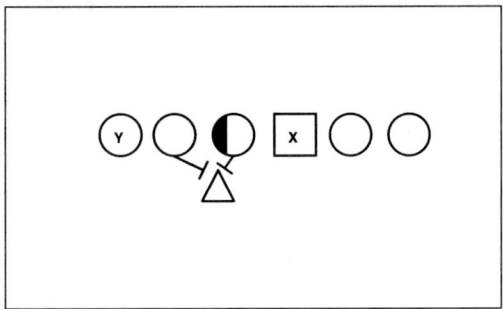

Figure 5-15. Double-team

As the defensive lineman feels continuous outside pressure, he should turn his shoulders perpendicular to the line of scrimmage. The defender should then drop the outside knee and shoulder to the drive man and split the seam. A low pad level is paramount. The defender tries to get the blockers on different levels by pulling himself upfield. Extending the driveside hip will serve to impede the drive man working to the next level. If the drive man stays on the block the defender should widen and hold the point on the line. As a last resort, defenders should create a pile by going to all fours or butt rolling to the drive man. Defensive linemen can't be driven off the line of scrimmage. The ability to defeat a double-team starts with pre-snap recognition. A definite giveaway is a reduced split.

Fold Blocks

A fold block is a combination block by two contiguous offensive linemen. It involves an angle block by one lineman, and a short pull by the other.

You can catalog fold blocks into three categories, or groups. If the angle block comes from the inside man it is referred to as an inside fold. Inside folds are used when the offense is trying to run inside or away from the inside shade defender. Figure 5-16 illustrates an inside fold, or George block.

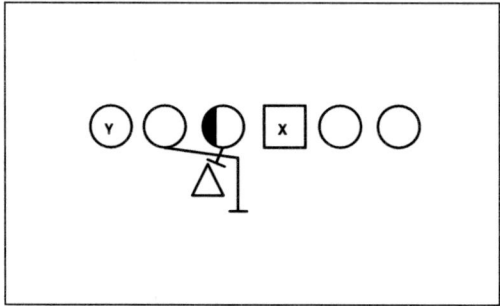

Figure 5-16. George block

An outside fold entails an angle block by the outside man and a short pull by the inside man. Figure 5-17 shows an outside fold, or tug block. An outside fold is usually executed on outside shades where the offense cannot control the outside shade with a reach or combo block.

The third category of fold blocks is a pull-collision block by the center for a guard which pulls across the ball. Figure 5-18 illustrates a turnback block.

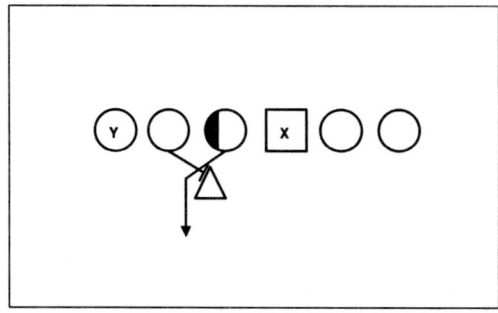

Figure 5-17. Tug block

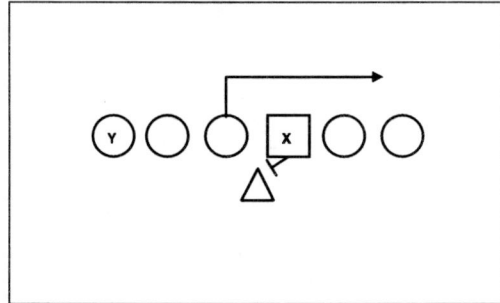

Figure 5-18. Pull-collision block

Defensive Fold Technique

The defensive response to use versus a fold block is exhibited in this section. If the man aligned on pulls either way, the defender should expect an angle block by the adjoining lineman in the direction of the pull. The defensive lineman will read the head of the angle blocker. If the blocker's head is too far upfield (toward the line of scrimmage) the defensive lineman will crossface. Figure 5-19 shows this reaction.

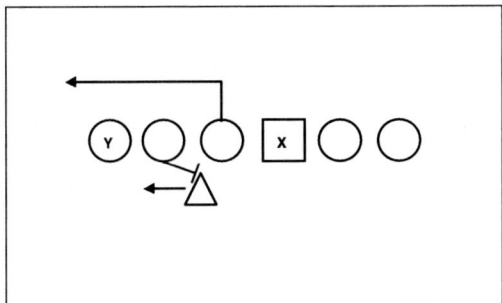

Figure 5-19. Defensive response versus fold block

Tip-offs to this blocking scheme include a tight guard-tackle split, or a staggered guard-tackle alignment. Many times the angle blocker crowds the line of scrimmage while the puller cushions his alignment (Figure 5-20).

If the angle blocker's head is too far downfield (away from the line of scrimmage), the defensive lineman will backdoor the play. This is called a half-moon technique. The defensive lineman will take his backside arm and grab the blocker's shoulder pad

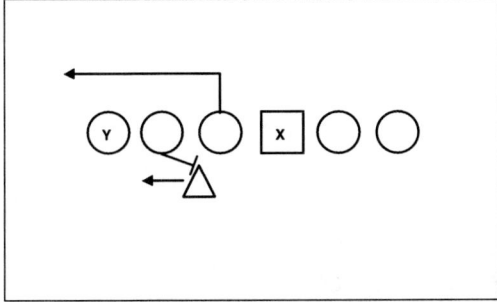

Figure 5-20. Staggered guard-tackle alignment

area and pivot around the block. The defender must work the blocker's heel line as he redirects, while ripping with his outside arm in a violent punch. This punch provides momentum and helps turn the defensive lineman's hips. The defender's back will end up facing the offensive side of the line of scrimmage. Figure 5-21 shows the half moon technique. If the blocker's head is in perfect position, the defender will play it like a base block and squeeze the adjacent hole using a steer technique (Figure 5-22).

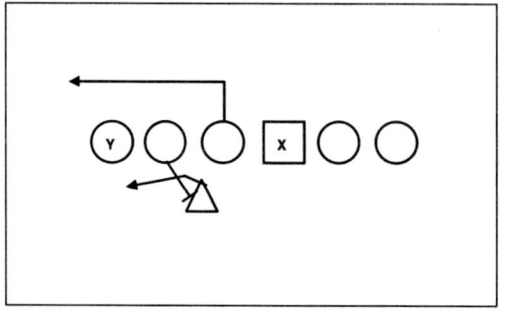

Figure 5-21. Half moon technique

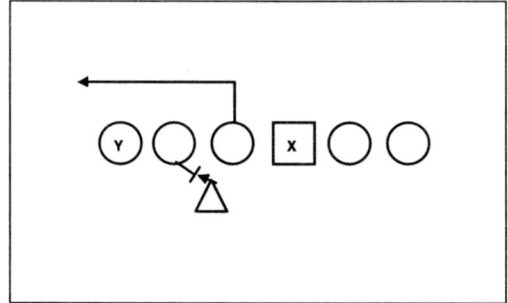

Figure 5-22. Squeezing adjacent hole with steer technique

Blocking Schemes Against Specific Shades

In this section, the shades outlined in Chapter 3 (Figure 3-21) will be covered in ascending order. The most commonly used blocks against these shades will be dissected and defensive counter measures explored. Included will be one-on-one and combination blocks. Each section will be broken down into playbook form.

0 Technique

Stance: Three-point

Alignment: Head-up, shoe-to-shoe on the center

Key: Ball

Execution: On ball movement attack the center. Shoot hands quickly and lockout elbows. Get hands inside and keep feet moving. Knock the center back.

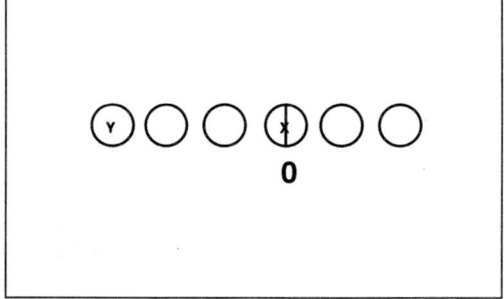

Figure 5-23. 0 technique

Responsibility:
- Run to: Frontside A gap
- Run away: Frontside A gap
- Pass: Game plan

Types of Blocks

Base (Figure 5-24): The defender should get his hands inside and drive the center straight back. He must be able to fall off to either side.

Reach (Figure 5-25): The defender should get hands on and lock out. He must get his hands inside and keep feet moving. He must knock the center back, and not be reached early. The linebacker can overlap the defender if he is reached late.

Double-team (Figure 5-26): The 0 technique must see both guards. When he feels a double-team, he should turn his shoulder to the drive blocker (guard). He should also drop his outside knee to the guard and try to split the seam. Extending the driveside hip will serve to impede the drive man from working to the next level. If the 0 technique feels movement he should, as a last resort, create a pile by going to all fours, or butt rolling to the drive man. The defender must not be driven off the line of scrimmage. The ability to defeat the double-team starts with pre-snap observation. A tip-off to a possible double-team will occur when the guard reduces his split.

Scoop (Figure 5-27): The initial stages of a scoop on the 0 technique will look very much like a reach block by the center. The defender should treat it as a reach block. As the 0 technique feels the center trying to slip off, he must keep his head in the crack. Grabbing the center will retard his route to the linebacker and will serve to propel him away from the backside guard. The 0 technique must not allow the backside guard to

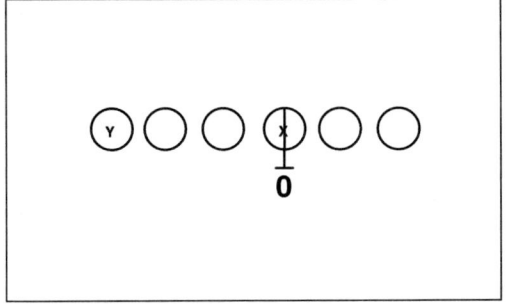

Figure 5-24. Base

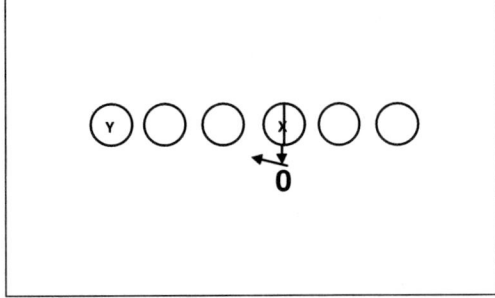

Figure 5-25. Reach

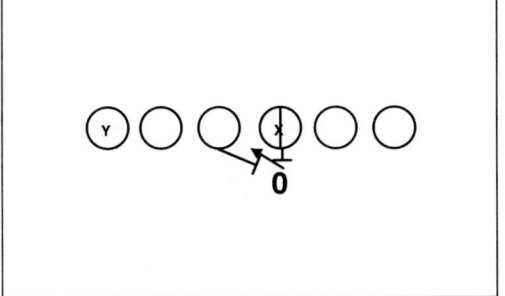

Figure 5-26. Double-team

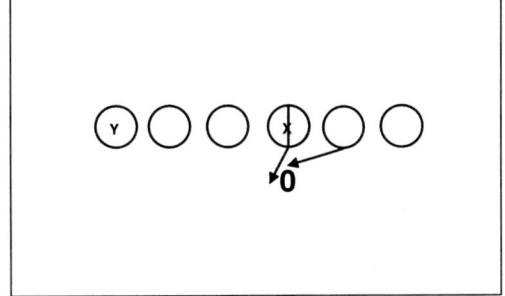

Figure 5-27. Scoop

get his head across. Thrusting the playside hip will serve to slow the center's release and will help the defender defeat the backside guard's block.

Back-Back (Figure 5-28): As the center steps flat, the defender may read this as a reach block. However, he will quickly discern that the center is not supplying any pressure to the defender. The center's shoulders—instead of staying parallel to the line of scrimmage—will be turned nearly perpendicular to the line. As the defender steps to meet the center, he will feel guard pressure. When he feels this pressure he should scotch and try to work vertically. He should try to gain penetration and grab any pullers who attempt to cross his face.

Slam-Back (Figure 5-29): In this case, the center bases, or chips, the defender before he blocks back. The 0 technique should fight the base, and when he feels the center leave and the guard pressure, he should get vertical. As he penetrates, he should grab any pulling linemen.

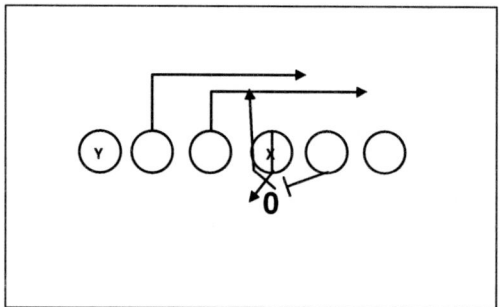

Figure 5-28. Back-back

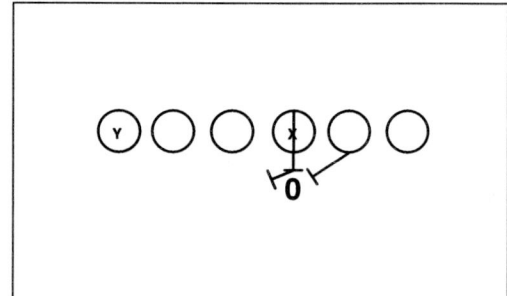

Figure 5-29. Slam-back

1 Technique

Stance: Three-point

Alignment: Inside foot on the center's crotch (ability level)

Key: Ball, center, and onside guard

Execution: On any movement attack the center

Responsibility:
- Run to: A gap. Expect double-team
- Run away: A gap
- Pass: A gap

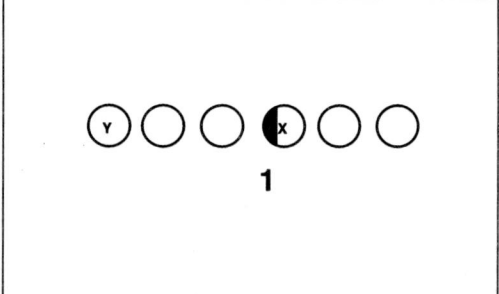

Figure 5-30. 1 technique

Types of Blocks

Base (Figure 5-31): The 1 technique should attack the V of the center's neck and claw the blocker maintaining A gap. He must get his head in the crack (HIC) and separate. He will hold leverage and squeeze the center playing a gap and a half while keeping the outside arm free for a bounce-out. The 1 technique must keep shoulders square to the line of scrimmage and fight pressure.

Center Turn-Back (Figure 5-32): The 1 technique will treat this as a base until he recognizes the guard is pulling. At this point, he should get upfield and try to grab a puller. If he's late, he should use the fold technique (Chapter 5).

Reach (Figure 5-33): The 1 technique will attack the V of the neck. He must get his hands out and elbows extended, trying to turn the center's shoulders to the sideline (long arm/short arm). The 1 technique will work him upfield, maintaining A gap by fighting pressure. A gap will expand as a result of the reach block. The defender must keep his outside arm free. He should flip his hips toward the reach.

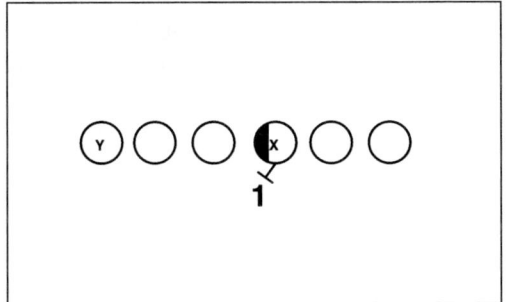

Figure 5-31. Base

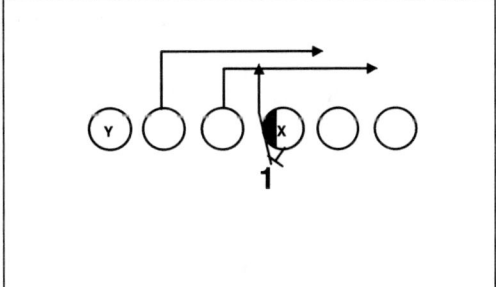

Figure 5-32. Center turn-back

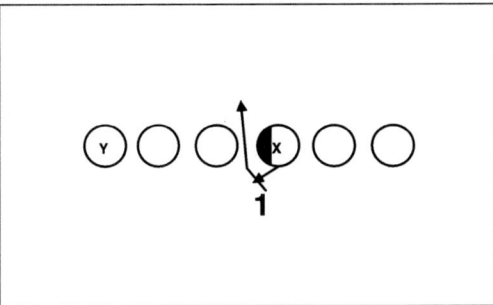

Figure 5-33. Reach

Pass (Figure 5-34): The 1 technique will read offensive lineman's high hat. The defender must gain ground on his first step. The 1 technique is responsible for the A gap rush lane. Seek to collapse the pocket. The 1 technique will probably be doubled by the center and guard. If the center oversets, the 1 technique can beat him through the backside A gap (Figure 5-35).

Turn-Back Pass Pro (Figure 5-36): The 1 technique will get the center's back or face, depending upon which way the protection is turned. If he gets the center's back, he can skinny through A gap or work across the guard's face. If he gets the center's face, with a high hat, he can skinny into frontside A, or B gap (Figure 5-37).

Double-Team (Figure 5-38): Penetration is the rule on a 1 technique double-team. The 1 technique should get his head in the crack (HIC), make his shoulders small, and split the double-team with his outside arm pulling his body upfield.

Wham (Figure 5-39): When the defender feels no pressure, he should freeze and identify the whammer, or trapper, and attack him.

Scoop (Figure 5-40): The 1 technique should attack the center, and feel the guard. He should hold on to the center as long as possible by grabbing the center, and accelerate his feet to keep the guard from taking over the block. He should keep the center off the linebacker and work to the frontside A gap.

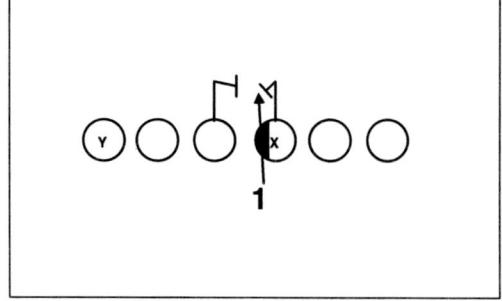

Figure 5-34. Pass

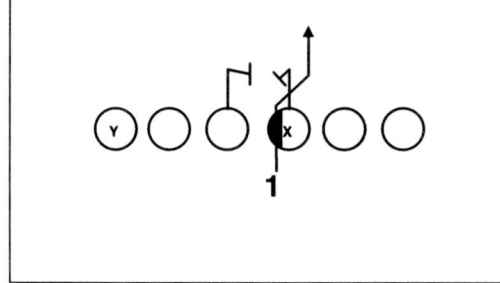

Figure 5-35. 1 technique versus oversetting center

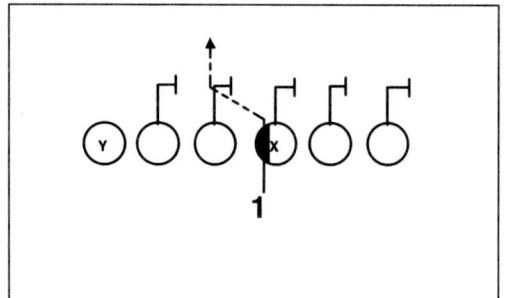

Figure 5-36. Turn-back pass pro

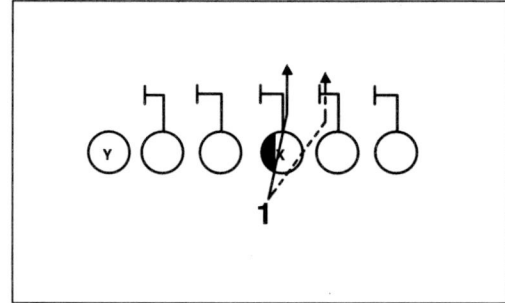

Figure 5-37. Skinny into frontside A or B gap

Figure 5-38. Double-team

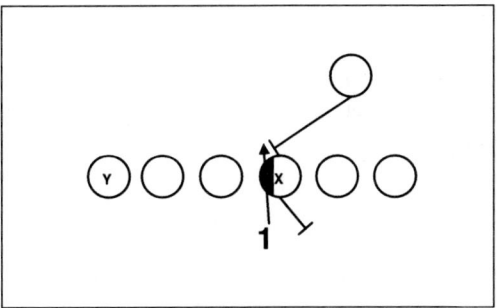

Figure 5-39. Wham

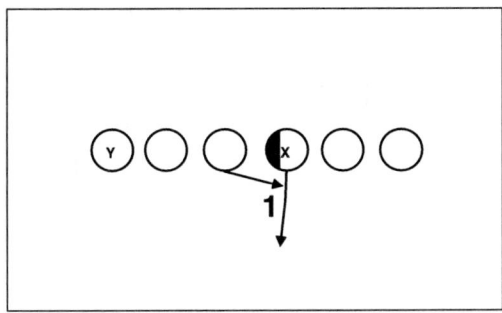

Figure 5-40. Scoop

2 Technique

Stance: Three-point

Alignment: Outside foot on the guard's crotch (ability level)

Key: Guard's hand, hat, and the ball (in his peripheral vision)

Execution: On any movement, attack the guard

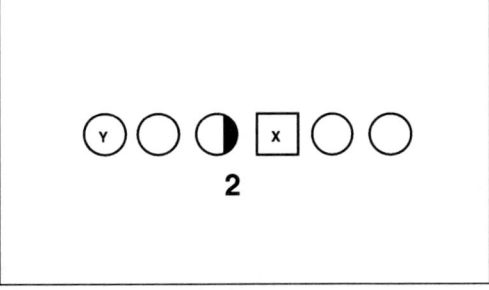

Figure 5-41. 2 technique

Responsibility:
- Run to: A gap
- Run away: Opposite A gap
- Pass: A gap

Types of Blocks

Base (Figure 5-42): This is the number one block to defeat. The defender attacks the inside shoulder of the guard and powers him upfield. He must hold the point. He cannot run around the block. He must fight pressure. The defender should use the steer technique. He should push with the outside hand on the pec and pull with the inside hand on the cuff.

Shoeshine (Figure 5-43): This block must be played from the ground up. The defender must keep the guard off his legs. The guard will seek to place his outside ear on the 2 technique's inside leg. The defender flattens the guard's head and tries to turn the blocker's shoulders perpendicular to the line of scrimmage. He should think fumbled snap to cutback.

Outside Release (Figure 5-44): The 2 technique must get back inside off the six-inch attack step. He should read the block of the center. If the center tries to reach him, the 2 technique will press him upfield. The 2 technique should spill any inside-out blocks.

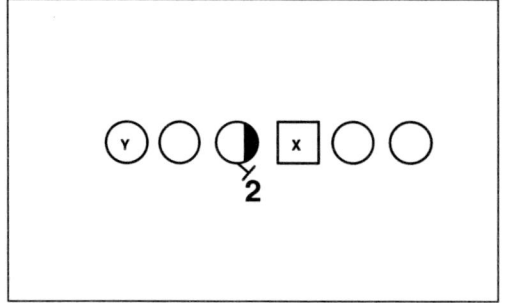

Figure 5-42. Base

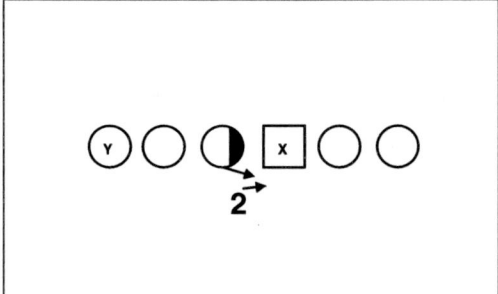

Figure 5-43. Shoeshine

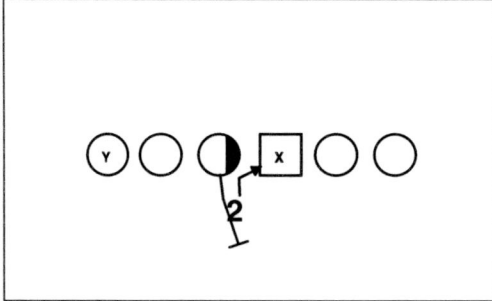

Figure 5-44. Outside release

Pass (Figure 5-45): The 2 technique reads offensive high hats. He must gain ground quickly while rushing A gap. He is responsible to try to collapse the pocket. The 2 technique will probably be doubled by the guard and center if the defense is in a base four man rush. If the center works away, the 2 technique has a two-way go on the guard (Figure 5-46). If the guard works away, and the center works to the 2 technique, he has a two-way go on the center (Figure 5-47). If the guard pass sets, and then pulls outside, the 2 technique should get his eyes inside to the pull lane. If the center is blocking at a flat angle away, close for a trap.

Down (Figure 5-48): The 2 technique will attack the V of the neck while keeping inside leverage. The defender must never allow the guard to crossface him. *This block should never be allowed to happen.*

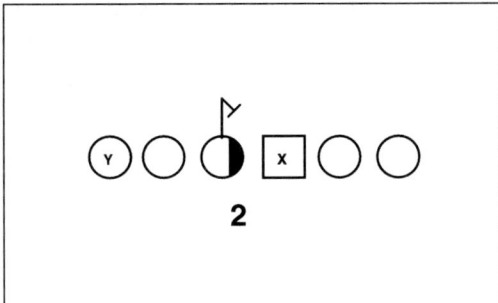

Figure 5-45. Pass

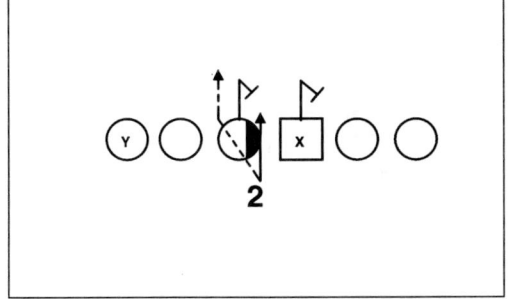

Figure 5-46. Two-way go on the guard

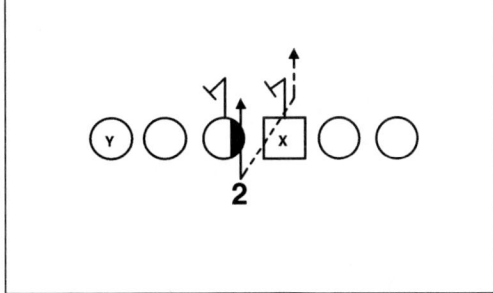

Figure 5-47. Two-way go on the center

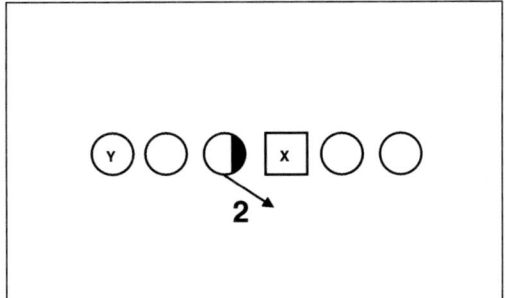

Figure 5-48. Down

Double (Figure 5-49): The defender should drive the guard into the backfield. The center will be negated if the 2 technique can get the center and guard on different levels.

Scoop (Figure 5-50): The 2 technique must not be driven off the line of scrimmage or allow the center a free release to the second level. If the defender can grab the slip blocker (center) with his playside hand, it would serve to keep the center off the linebacker and propel the defender away from the guard. The 2 technique should stay low, and work to stay in the crease keeping his playside arm and leg free.

Zone (Figure 5-51): The guard may release outside or rub the 2 technique as he works to the second level. If the guard outside releases, the 2 technique gets his eyes inside on the center. If the center is attacking with a flat head, he should push off him with hands and pursue down the line of scrimmage. If the guard seeks to chip, or rub, the 2 technique will treat it as a base or double-team. He must take the fight to the guard. As he feels the guard leaving, he must fight to keep his head in the crack. He should throw his hips to the outside.

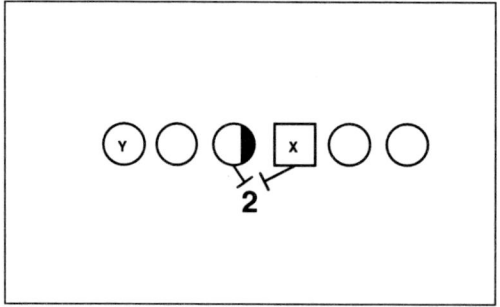
Figure 5-49. Double

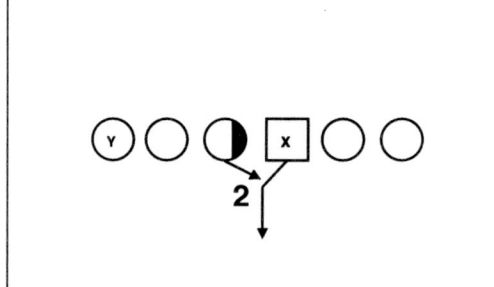
Figure 5-50. Scoop

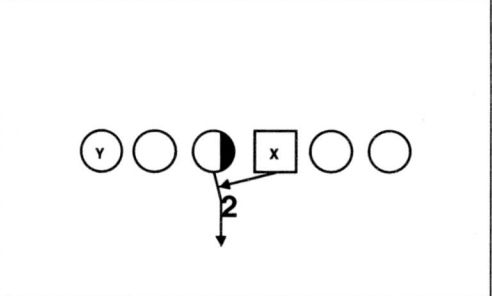
Figure 5-51. Zone

Guard Pulling Across the Ball (Figure 5-52): As the 2 technique attacks the guard, the guard pulls crossing the ball. In this case, the defender takes his eyes to the center. The 2 technique will react to the center's head placement. If the center's head is too flat the defender will crossface (Figure 5-53). If the center's check-back block is too far behind the 2 technique, he will half moon, or backdoor the play. The defender must redirect tight off the center's heel line as he pursues the ball (Figure 5-54).

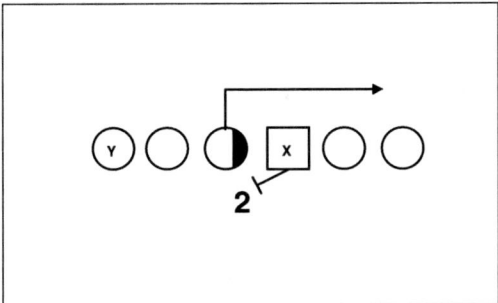

Figure 5-52. Guard pulling across the ball

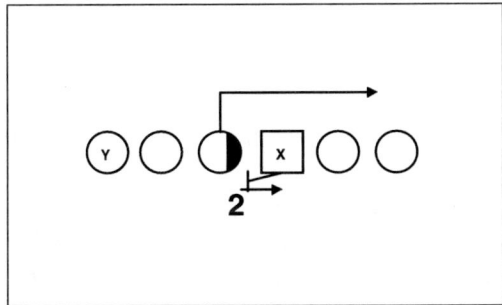

Figure 5-53. Crossing center's face

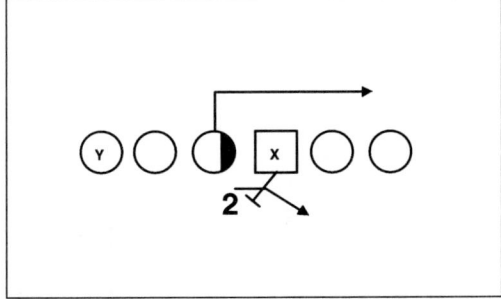

Figure 5-54. Redirecting off center's heel line

3 Technique

Stance: Three-point

Alignment: Inside foot on the guard's crotch (ability level)

Key: Guard's hand, hat, and the ball (in his peripheral vision)

Execution: On any movement attack the guard

Responsibility:
- Run to: B gap
- Run away: Collapse to A gap
- Pass: B gap

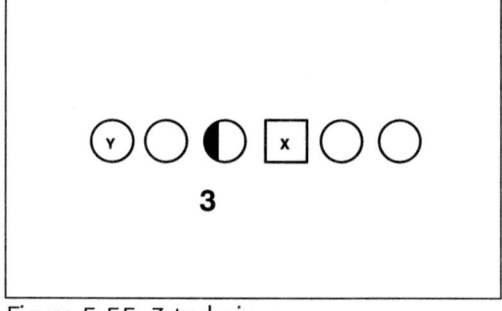

Figure 5-55. 3 technique

Types of Blocks

Base (Figure 5-56): This is the number one block to defeat. The defender attacks the V of the guard's neck. He claws the guard by getting his hands inside. He must keep his weight on the balls of the feet and create a new line of scrimmage by knocking the blocker back. He must hold the point. He cannot open up A gap by running upfield. He must maintain B gap by fighting pressure using a steer technique. He should push on the guard's pec with his inside hand and turn the guard's outside shoulder inside with his outside hand on the cuff. He tries to keep his shoulders square to the line of scrimmage. He must keep his feet moving and expect the ball to bounce-out to B gap. The 3 technique is primarily responsible for the area head-up to the outside. Secondary responsibility involves squeezing A gap, making the hole smaller.

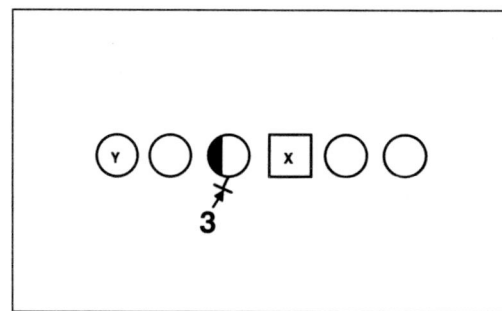

Figure 5-56. Base

Down (Figure 5-57): The defender will squeeze, and replace the guard. He tries to get his outside hand on the guard's hip or base of the numbers. He thinks dive to pull lane. He will spill any inside-out blocks. If it is a jump-through scheme, the defender must avoid the offensive tackle's shoeshine block.

Down/Down (Figure 5-58): The defender will play trap or dive until he feels tackle pressure. At this point, he should get upfield and grab any pulling linemen. He must play trap first and then react to the outside pressure.

Trap (Figure 5-59): The 3 technique will claw the guard with eyes looking into the pull lane. When the 3 technique reads the trap, he will throw his outside shoulder at the inside thigh of the trapper. He should stay on his feet and reach with his inside arm to tackle the ballcarrier while squaring up on the blocker. The wrong arm must not occur flat on the line of scrimmage. Any defender spilling an inside-out block should press slightly upfield off the line of scrimmage to make the ball carrier bounce or run the hump.

Reach (Figure 5-60): The 3 technique attacks the guard's outside shoulder using hands and a lockout. Turn the blocker's shoulders toward the sideline using a long arm/short arm technique (steer technique). The 3 technique will work to the spot (2x1) driving the guard upfield. He must set the point. A key to defeating a reach block is to attack the blocker when the ball is snapped. Another key is to keep the defender's hips outside. Versus a jump-reach the defender should regain initial positioning without committing outside too quickly. He will force the guard upfield and anticipate falling back inside should the ball cut back.

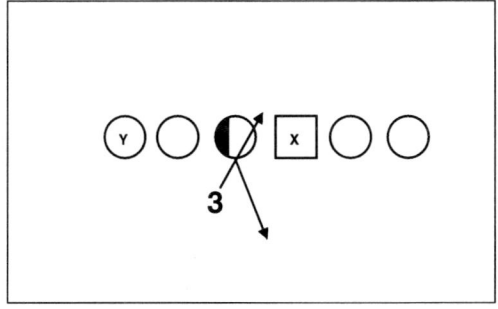

Figure 5-57. Down

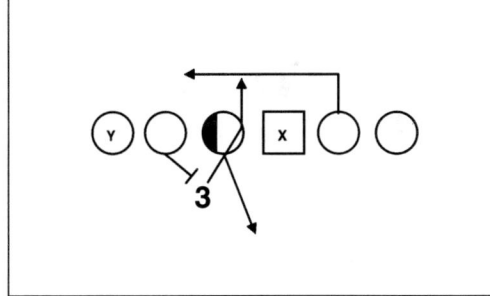

Figure 5-58. Down/down

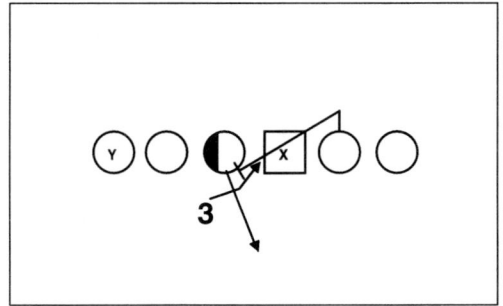

Figure 5-59. Trap

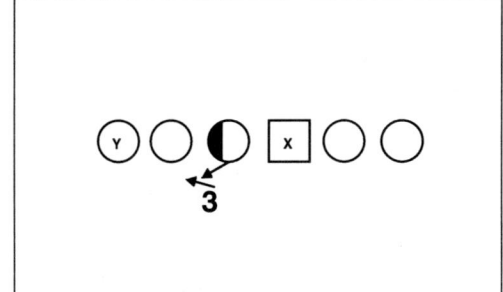

Figure 5-60. Reach

Cut Reach: If the blocker drives his head below the knee level of the defender, the defender should drive the blocker's head down and away. Giving a little ground is permissible to keep the outside leg free. The defender cannot allow the offensive lineman to leverage his outside leg.

Pass (Figure 5-61): The defender must read a high hat and gain ground quickly. He will rush B gap trying to collapse the pocket. The 3 technique has the availability of a two-way go, especially if the guard sets hard outside.

Draw (Figure 5-62): An exaggerated shoulder turn, and highly active hands from the guard should serve as a tip-off. When the defender reads draw, he should press the guard to squeeze the hole and then retrace his steps back to the line of scrimmage.

Zone (Figure 5-63): The defensive lineman should drop his outside shoulder underneath the offensive tackle and drive into him. A contributing factor which can be beneficial to the 3 technique is how fast the linebacker scrapes over the top. The faster and more downhill a linebacker runs, the harder it will be for the offensive tackle to get to him. As a result, the tackle will have to climb to the second level quickly. If the linebacker is slow, the offensive tackle can stay on the 3 technique longer before he works to the second level. The defender must know the difference between a zone and a true double-team block. If the defender misreads the zone and thinks it is a double, he may collapse and allow the offensive tackle to work up to the second level.

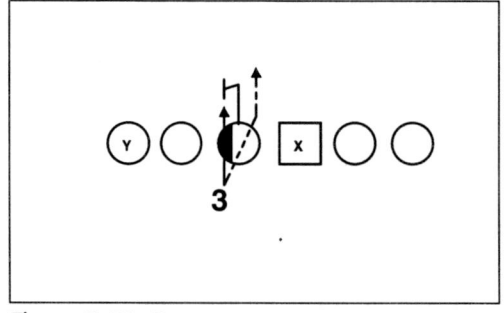

Figure 5-61. Pass

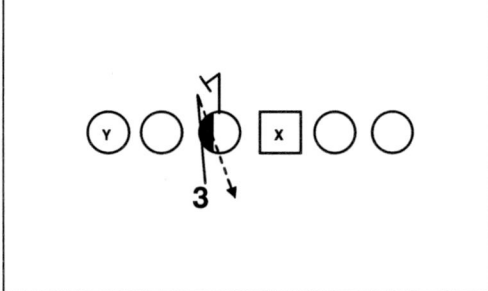

Figure 5-62. Draw

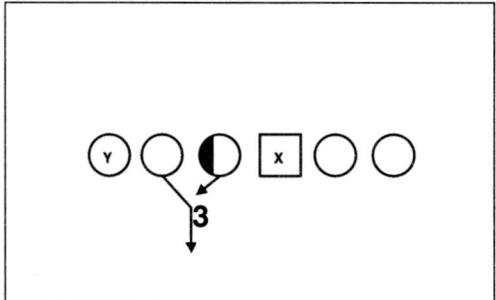

Figure 5-63. Zone

Double (Figure 5-64): As the 3 technique feels the double-team, he should swivel his hips to the offensive tackle and turn his shoulders perpendicular to the line of scrimmage. He should drop his outside knee with a low pad level and try to split the double-team. He must not allow the tackle to work up to the second level. The defender's two main objectives should be to not get knocked off the ball and to occupy two blockers. The defender must fight to keep his head in the crack (i.e., the gap between the two blockers).

Wham (Figure 5-65): Early on, this block will appear to be a trap block. If no one traps or zones quickly, the defender should get his eyes into the backfield for the whammer. If the defender feels air, he needs to look for wham.

Guard Pulls Inside With the Center Turning Back (Figure 5-66): The 3 technique should use the fold technique. If the center's angle block has his head behind the 3 technique's hip the 3 technique can backdoor or half moon the play (Figure 5-67). If the center's head is in front of the defender, the defender can crossface (Figure 5-68). If the head position from the center is perfect, the defender will play it like a base and squeeze the adjacent hole.

Guard Pulls Outside With the Tackle Angle Blocking (Figure 5-69): The defender should get his eyes inside for the influence trap. As he reads the offensive tackle's pressure, he should check for the blocker's head position. If the tackle's head is upfield, the defender can crossface (Figure 5-70). If the blocker's head is downfield, the defender can backdoor the play (Figure 5-71). If the offensive tackle's head is perfect, the defender will treat it like a base block and squeeze B gap with the blocker's body.

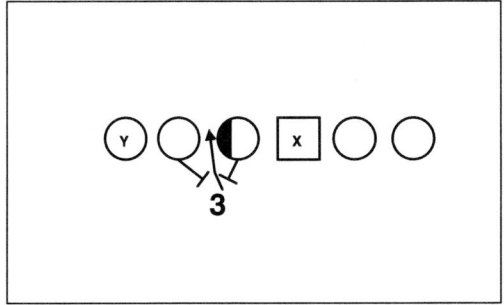

Figure 5-64. Double

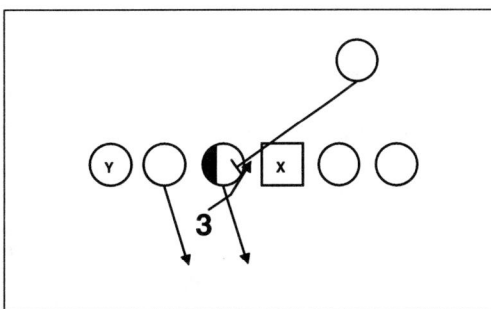

Figure 5-65. Wham

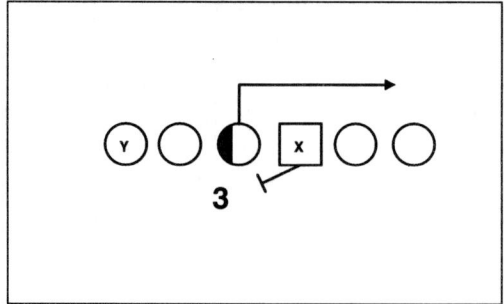

Figure 5-66. Guard pulls inside with the center turning back

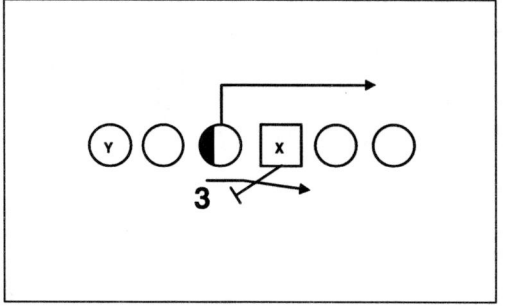

Figure 5-67. Half moon

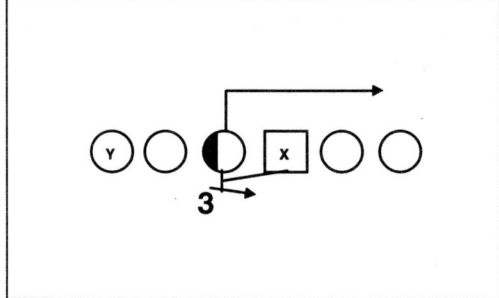

Figure 5-68. Crossface

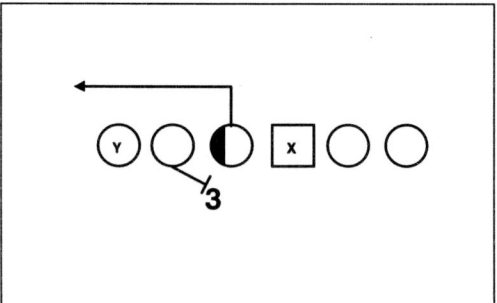

Figure 5-69. Guard pulls outside with the tackle angle blocking

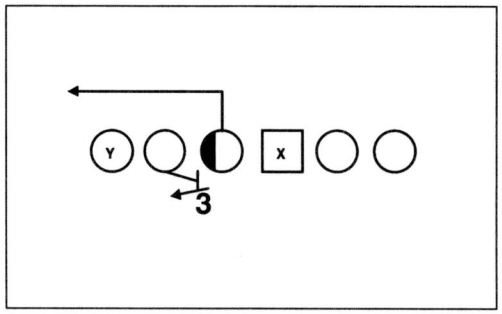

Figure 5-70. Crossface

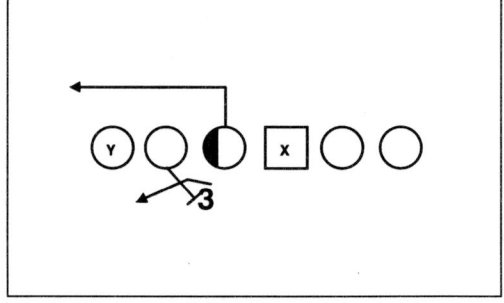

Figure 5-71. Backdoor

4 Technique

Stance: Three-point

Alignment: Outside foot on the tackle's crotch (ability level)

Key: Tackle's hand, hat, guard, and the ball (in his peripheral vision)

Execution: On any movement, attack the tackle

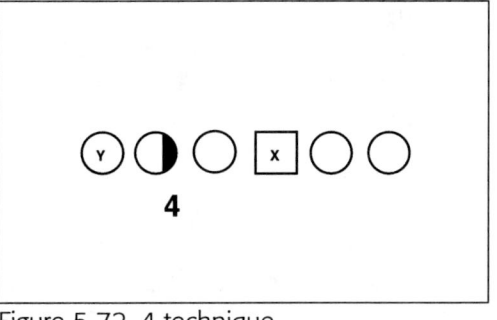

Figure 5-72. 4 technique

Responsibility:
- Run to: B gap
- Run away: Close to A gap
- Pass: B gap

Types of Blocks

Base (Figure 5-73): This is the number one block to defeat. The 4 technique will attack the inside shoulder of the tackle and power him back upfield. He must hold the point. The defender cannot run around the block, he must fight pressure. He should use the steer technique. This involves pushing with the outside hand on the blocker's pec and pulling with the inside hand on the blocker's inside cuff.

Shoeshine (Figure 5-74): This block must be played from the ground up. The defender must keep the tackle off his legs. The tackle will seek to place his outside ear on the 4 technique's inside leg. The defender will flatten the tackle's head and try to turn the blocker's shoulders perpendicular to the line of scrimmage. The 4 technique should think fumbled snap to cutback.

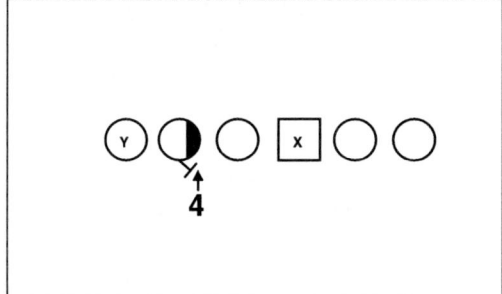

Figure 5-73. Base

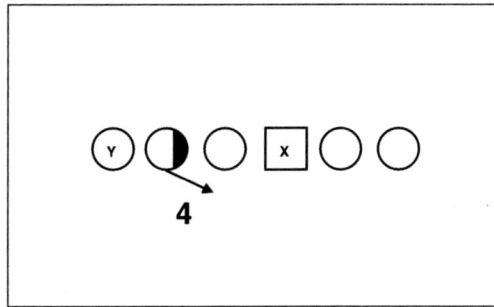

Figure 5-74. Shoeshine

Outside Release (Figure 5-75): The 4 technique will get back inside off his six-inch attack step. He will read the block of the guard. If the guard reaches, press him upfield. Spill any inside-out blocks. Some teams will influence trap the 4 technique by having the guard pass set, then pull outside. In this case the 4 technique should get his eyes inside to the center. If the center is blocking at a flat angle away, the 4 technique should close for a trap.

Pass (Figure 5-76): The 4 technique will read offensive high hats and gain ground quickly. He will rush B gap and try to collapse the pocket. The 4 technique has a straight line to the quarterback. The offensive tackle must not be able to block him effectively by himself. If the guard blocks the defender with the tackle finding work elsewhere, the 4 technique has a two-way go on the guard (Figure 5-77).

Down (Figure 5-78): The 4 technique will attack the V of the neck. The defender must keep inside leverage. He cannot allow the tackle to cross his face. *This block should never be allowed to happen.*

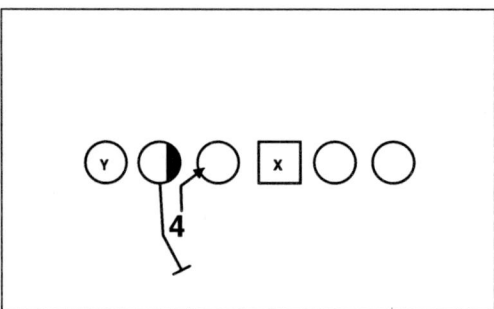

Figure 5-75. Outside release

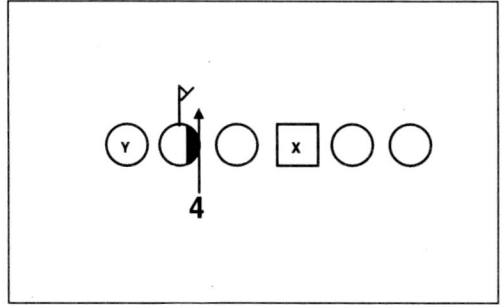

Figure 5-76. Pass

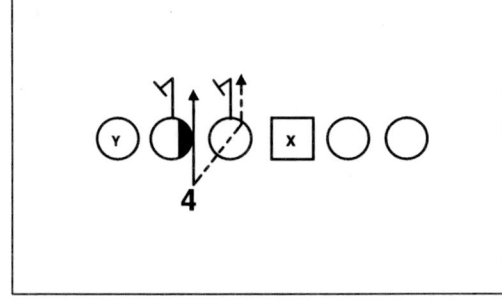

Figure 5-77. Two-way go

Double (Figure 5-79): The 4 technique will drive the tackle into the backfield. The guard will be negated if the defender can get them on different levels.

Scoop (Figure 5-80): The defender must not be driven off the line of scrimmage, nor should he allow the guard a free release to the second level. If the defender can grab the slip blocker (guard) with his playside hand, it would serve to keep the guard off the linebacker and propel the defender away from the offensive tackle. The 4 technique should stay low and work to stay in the crease keeping his playside arm and leg free.

Zone (Figure 5-81): The offensive tackle may outside release, or rub to the second level. If the tackle outside releases, the 4 technique must get his eyes inside on the guard. If the guard is attacking with a flat head, the defender pushes off him with hands and pursues down the line of scrimmage. If the tackle seeks to chip or rub treat it as a base or double-team. The defender should take the fight to the tackle. As the 4 technique feels the tackle leaving, he will fight to keep his head in the crack. He should throw hips to the outside.

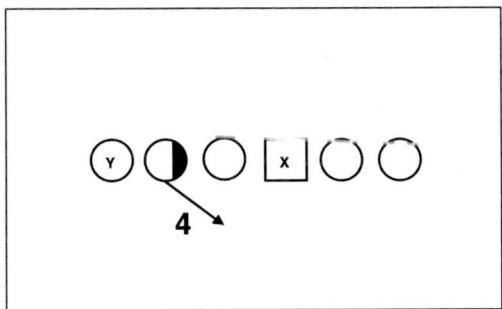

Figure 5-78. Down

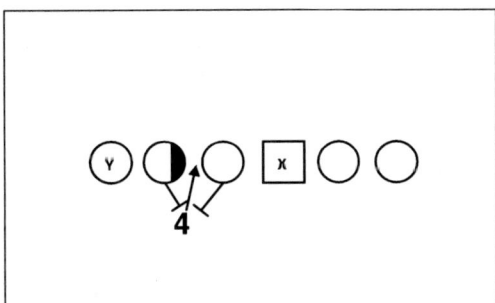

Figure 5-79. Double

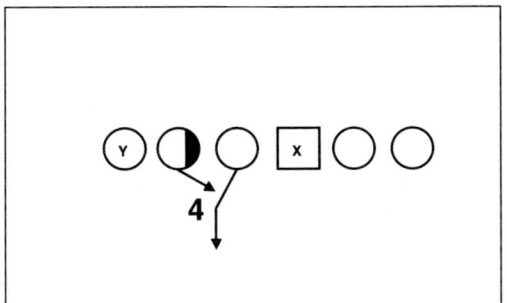

Figure 5-80. Scoop

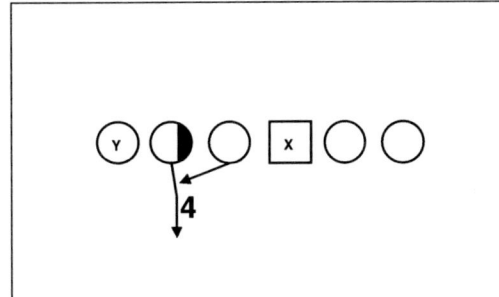

Figure 5-81. Zone

Tackle Pulling With the Guard Angle Blocking (Figure 5-82): This inside fold—or George block—consists of a tackle pulling inside and the guard angle blocking. When the offensive tackle pulls inside, the defender should take his eyes to the guard. If the guard's head is behind the defensive tackle's hip, he can backdoor or half moon the guard, staying close to the guard's heels (Figure 5-83). If the guard's head is in front of the 4 technique he can crossface the blocker (Figure 5-84). If the guard's head is in the correct spot, the defender should treat this as a base block and squeeze the adjacent gap with the guard's body (Figure 5-85).

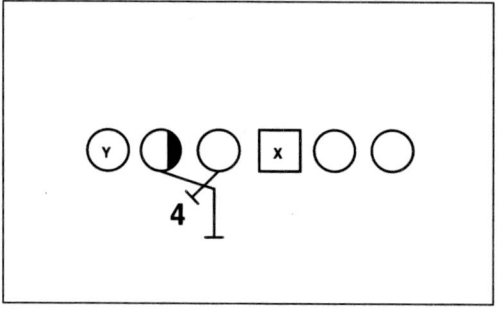

Figure 5-82. Tackle pulling with the guard angle blocking

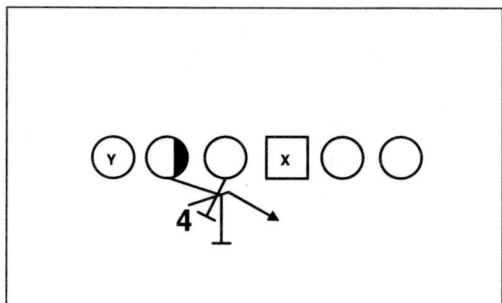

Figure 5-83. Half moon

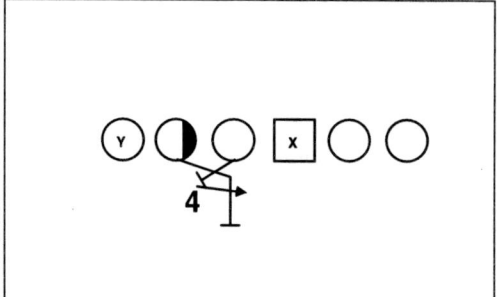

Figure 5-84. Crossface

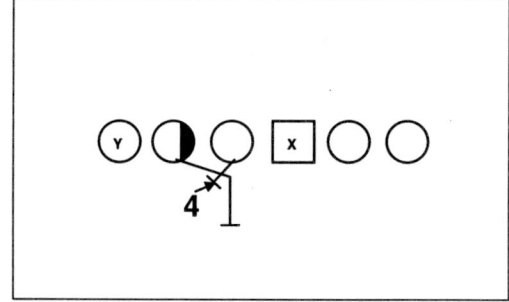

Figure 5-85. Squeezing adjacent gap

5 Technique

Stance: Three-point

Alignment: Inside foot on the tackle's crotch (ability level)

Key: Tackle's hand, hat, and the ball (in his peripheral vision)

Execution: On any movement, attack the tackle

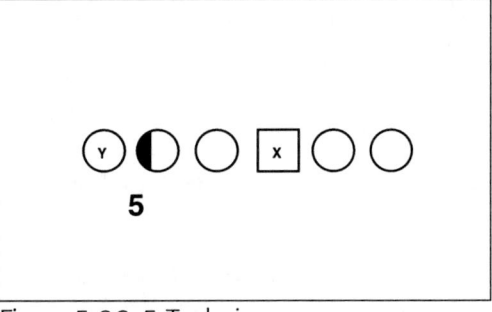

Figure 5-86. 5 Technique

Responsibility:
- Run to: C gap
- Run away: Collapse to B gap
- Pass: C gap (possible cage)

Types of Blocks

Base (Figure 5-87): This is the number one block to defeat. The defender will attack the V of the tackle's neck. He will claw the tackle by getting his hands inside. He will keep his weight on the balls of his feet and create a new line of scrimmage by knocking the blocker back. He must hold the point. He cannot open up B gap by running upfield. He must maintain C gap by fighting pressure using a steer technique. He will push on the tackle's pec with his inside hand, and turn the blocker's outside shoulder inside with his outside hand on the blocker's outside cuff. He must keep his feet moving and expect the ball to bounce out to C gap. The 5 technique is primarily responsible for the area head-up to the outside. Secondary responsibility involves squeezing B gap making the hole smaller.

Down (Figure 5-88): The 5 technique will squeeze and replace the tackle. He will attempt to get his outside hand on the guard's hip or base of the numbers. The defender thinks dive to pull lane. He will spill any inside-out blocks. If the scheme is a jump-through the defender must avoid the tight end's shoeshine block.

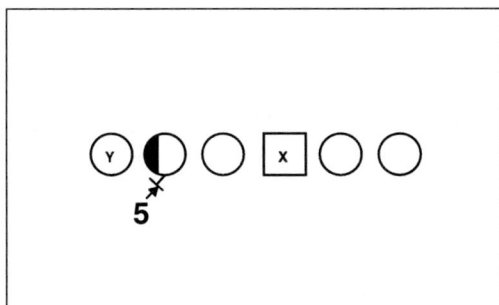

Figure 5-87. Base

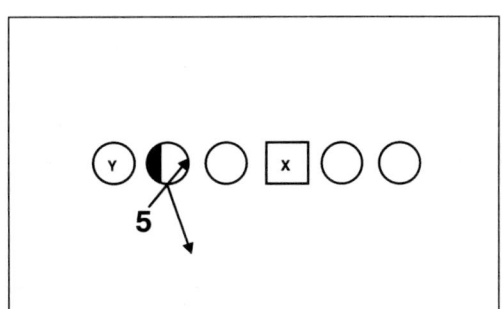

Figure 5-88. Down

Down/Down (Figure 5-89): The defender will play trap or dive until he feels pressure from the end. At this point, he should get upfield and grab any pulling linemen. He should play trap and dive first and then react to the outside pressure.

Trap (Figure 5-90): The 5 technique will claw the tackle with eyes into the pull lane. When the defender reads the trap, he will throw his outside arm at the inside thigh of the trapper. The 5 technique must stay on his feet and reach with his inside arm to tackle the ballcarrier while squaring up on the blocker.

Reach (Figure 5-91): The 5 technique will attack the tackle's outside shoulder using hands and lockout. He will then turn the blocker's shoulders toward the sideline using a long arm/short arm technique (steer technique). The 5 technique will work to the spot (4x1), driving the tackle upfield. Set a point. The key is to attack the man when the ball is snapped—beat him to the punch! Another key is to keep the hips outside. Versus a jump-reach, the defender should regain initial positioning without committing outside too quickly. He should force the tackle upfield and anticipate falling back inside should the ball cut back.

Cut Reach: If the blocker drives his head below the knee level of the defender, the defender should drive the blocker's head down and away. Giving a little ground is permissible to keep the outside leg free. The defender cannot allow the offensive lineman to leverage his outside leg.

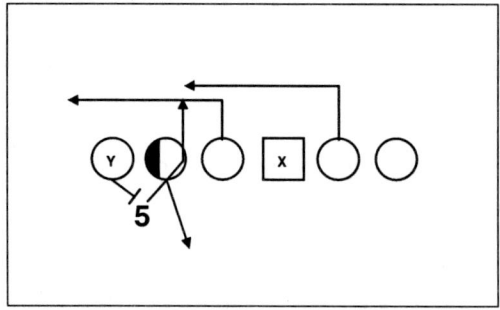

Figure 5-89. Down/down

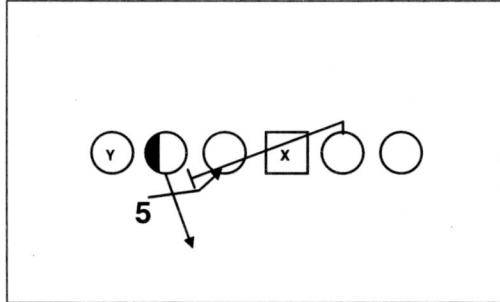

Figure 5-90. Trap

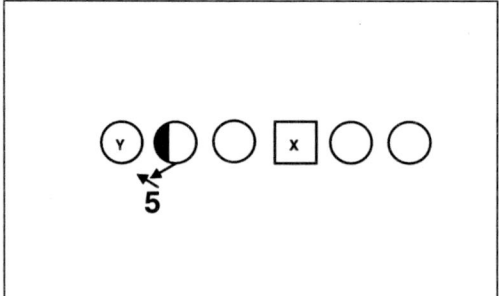

Figure 5-91. Reach

Pass (Figure 5-92): The defender must read a high hat and gain ground quickly. He is responsible for C gap. As a basic rule, the 5 technique has cage on the quarterback. However, an outside stunter makes the 5 technique "hot". The defender, in this case, can go under a pass set (Figure 5-93).

Draw (Figure 5-94): An exaggerated shoulder turn and highly active hands by the offensive tackle should serve as a tip-off. When the defender reads draw, he should press the tackle to squeeze hole and retrace his steps back to the line of scrimmage.

Zone (Figure 5-95): The key to playing this scheme is similar to the double-team technique. The defensive lineman should drop his outside shoulder underneath the offensive end and drive into him. A factor which can be beneficial to the 5 technique is how fast the linebacker scrapes over the top. The faster and more downhill a linebacker runs, the harder it will be for the tight end to get to him. If the backer is slow, the tight end can stay on the 5 technique longer before he works to the second level. The defender must know the difference between a zone and a true double-team block. If the defender misreads the zone and thinks it is a double, he may collapse and allow the tight end to work up to the second level.

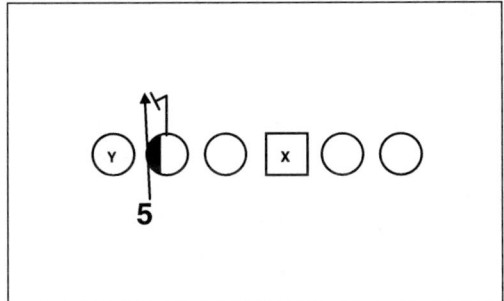

Figure 5-92. Pass

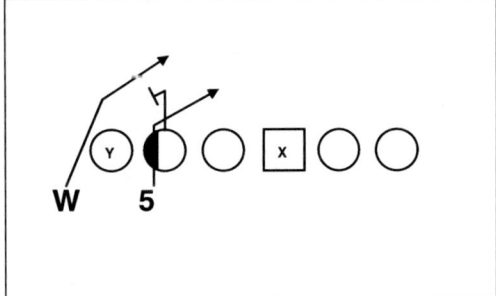

Figure 5-93. Under a pass set

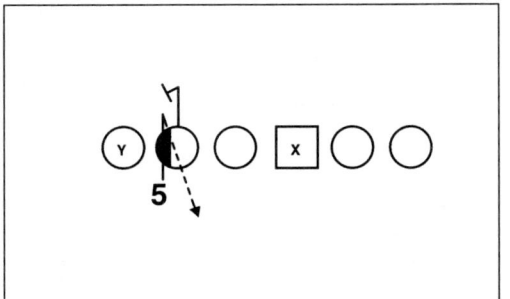

Figure 5-94. Draw

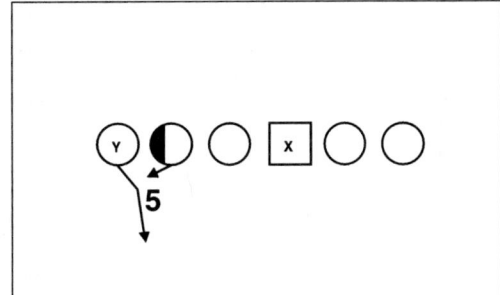

Figure 5-95. Zone

Double (Figure 5-96): As the 5 technique feels the double-team, he should swivel his hips to the tight end and turn his shoulders perpendicular to the line of scrimmage. He should drop his outside knee with a low pad level and try to split the double-team. He must not allow the end to work up to the second level. The defender's two main objectives would be to not get knocked off the ball as well as occupying two blockers.

Wham (Figure 5-97): At the inception of the play, the wham block will appear to be a trap block. If no one traps or zones, the defender should get his eyes into the backfield for the whammer. If the defender feels air, he needs to look for wham.

Tackle Pulls Outside With the End Angle Blocking (Figure 5-98): The defender should get his eyes inside for the influence trap. As he reads the offensive end's pressure, he should check for the blocker's head position. If the end's head is upfield the defender can crossface (Figure 5-99). If the blocker's head is downfield the defender can backdoor the play (Figure 5-100). If the tight end's head is perfect, the defender will treat it like a base block and squeeze D gap with the blocker's body.

Tackle Pulls Inside (Open End) (Figure 5-101): The 5 technique will check the back for his intentions. If the back seal blocks or check blocks the 5 technique will spill and chase (Figure 5-102). If the back slam releases, the 5 technique will get depth and width checking for bootleg (Figure 5-103).

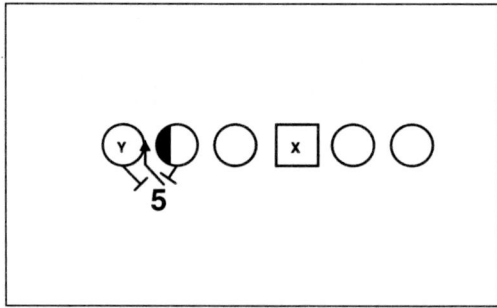

Figure 5-96. Double

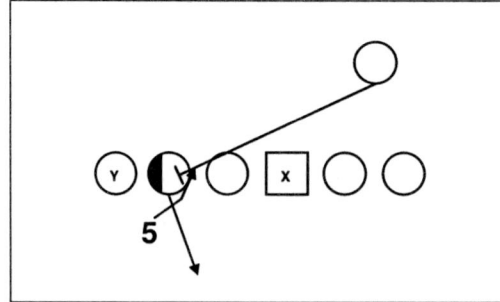

Figure 5-97. Wham

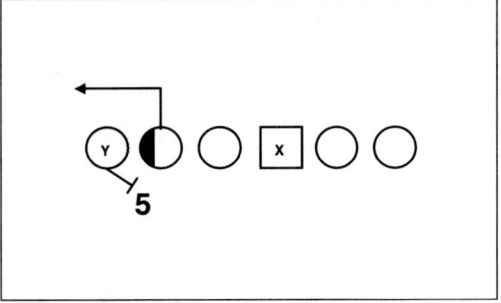

Figure 5-98. Tackle pulls outside with the end angle blocking

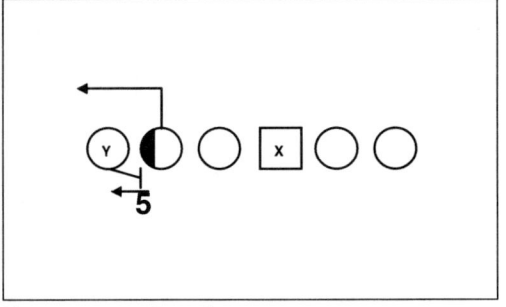

Figure 5-99. Crossface

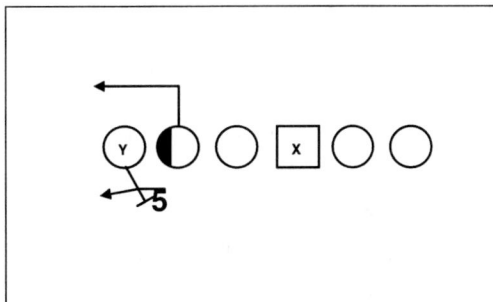

Figure 5-100. Backdoor

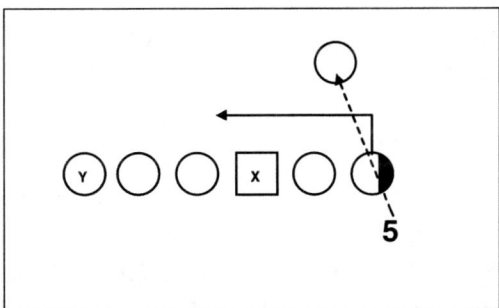

Figure 5-101. Tackle pulls inside (open end)

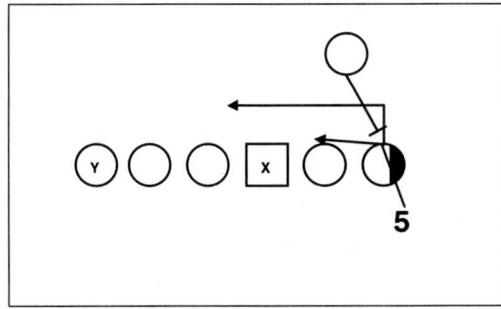

Figure 5-102. Spill and chase

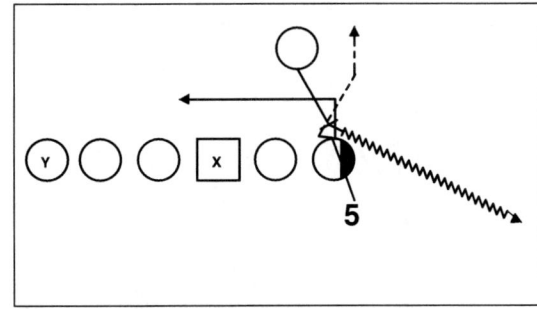

Figure 5-103. Get depth and width

6 Technique

Stance: Three-point

Alignment: Head up, foot-to-foot on the tight end versus normal split (up to four feet from the offensive tackle). If the tight end splits more than four yards the 6 technique will move to a 7 technique.

Key: The tight end's hand, hat, and the ball (in his peripheral vision)

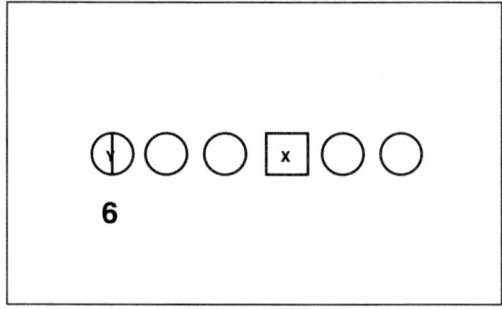

Figure 5-104. 6 technique

Execution: On any movement, attack the tight end. Dominate the tight end.

Responsibility:
- Run to: C gap
- Run away: Chase
- Pass: Late cage on quarterback

Types of Blocks

Base (Figure 5-105): This is the number one block to defeat. Explode into, and whip, the tight end. The 6 technique must be pad-under-pad with his hands inside. He must stay square and drive the blocker back until the ball declares. He must keep the blocker's shoulders square. Don't allow the blocker to gain inside or outside leverage. The 6 technique can't pick a side. The 6 technique must take on any threat in C gap.

Down (Figure 5-106): The 6 technique should knock the tight end off course. The defender tries to flatten the end down the line. The 6 technique must not overpenetrate. The 6 technique should stay square with his eyes inside to the pull lane. Close off C gap. Don't allow air between self and the tight end. The 6 technique can either take on inside-out blocks with an inside shoulder squeeze technique or an outside shoulder spill technique, whatever the coach prefers.

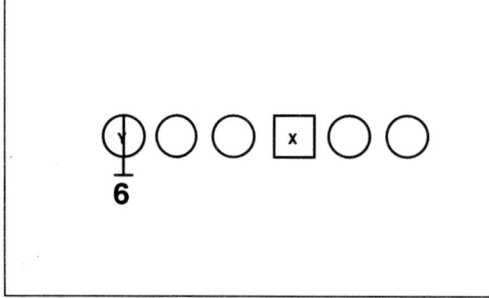

Figure 5-105. Base

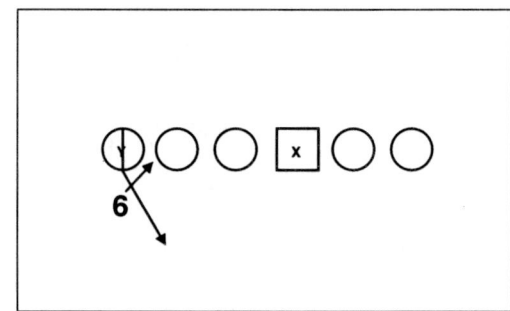

Figure 5-106. Down

Reach (Figure 5-107): The 6 technique will press the tight end inside-out anchoring C gap while looking for the ball to cutback. The 6 technique will beat the hook block by squeezing the blocker outside. The defender will drive him off the line of scrimmage by squeezing him upfield. If the 6 technique sees the ball inside he can penetrate underneath but he must ensure the tackle. He only crossfaces the blocker when the ball crosses his face. Under no circumstances should the defender be knocked back as this would cut off pursuit.

Co-Op Block (Figure 5-108): The tight end will reach the 6 technique and then slip off to the second level with the offensive tackle cleaning up. The 6 technique must explode into the tight end. Never allow the offensive tackle to reach the 6 technique.

Cut-Off Block (High Wall) (Figure 5-109): The tight end's head will be in C gap. The block at its inception will look like a down block except the tight end will high wall the 6 technique. The 6 technique should squeeze the blocker and close C gap with the blocker's body. He must not get knocked off the line of scrimmage. The 6 technique has reverse responsibilities. The 6 technique can crossface the blocker if he sees the ball inside.

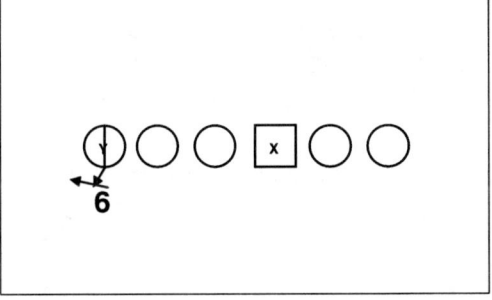

Figure 5-107. Reach

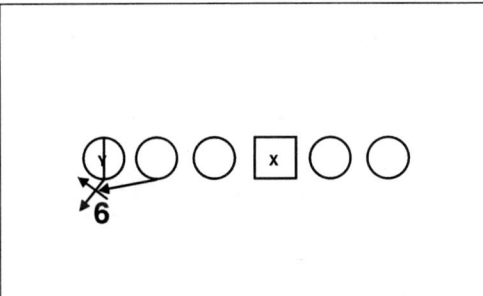

Figure 5-108. Co-op block

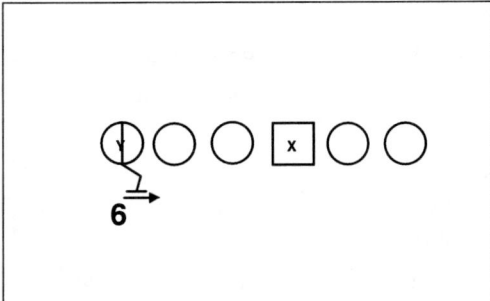

Figure 5-109. Cut-off block (high wall)

Out/Out (Figure 5-110): Once the tight end declares his block on an outside defender the 6 technique must get his eyes back inside on the offensive tackle. He should attack the tackle outside-in. The 6 technique should use a push/pull technique to work back square to the line of scrimmage. He should push with his inside hand and pull with his outside hand. He should keep his shoulders square to the line of scrimmage for a bounce-out. He shouldn't run upfield. The 6 technique should squeeze C gap with his outside leg back, and stay pad-under-pad.

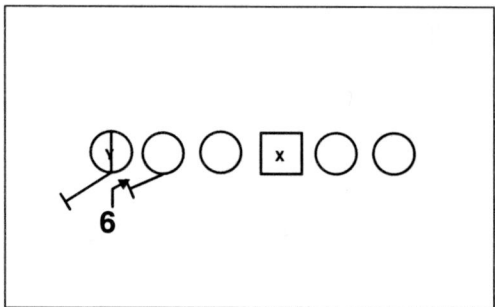

Figure 5-110. Out/out

Outside Release (Figure 5-111): The 6 technique should respect the initial angle of the tight end. It looks like a reach block. The 6 technique should ride the tight end with his hands and locate the second blocking threat. Possibilities off an outside release include:

- Near Back Kick Out (Figure 5-112): When the 6 recognizes the back on an inside-out course he should drive off his outside foot and attack the back. The 6 should spill or wrong arm the block making the play bounce outside. He must get his head into C gap and not run up field.

- Guard Kick Out (Figure 5-113): The 6 technique will spill, or wrong arm the guard's block forcing the ball to bounce. The 6 technique must get his head into C gap and not run upfield or get kicked out.

- Option (Figure 5-114): When the 6 technique reads an outside release, he takes his eyes to the pull lane. When he reads down the line action, he will close and take the first threat.

- Pass (Figure 5-115): When the defender's eyes get back inside to the pull lane, he will see a pass set by the offensive tackle. The 6 technique will have cage responsibility on the quarterback.

- Sprint Pass (Figure 5-116): The tackle will turn back, or reach/punch and then turn back. The 6 technique must know the difference between a kick-out or pin block by the onside back. A kick-out block will threaten the 6 technique's inside shoulder, while a pin or load block will seek to leverage the outside shoulder. The 6 technique must *feel* the fullback and *see* the tailback. He must protect his outside leg and outside pad. He should pull up the quarterback as soon as possible and *never* allow him outside.

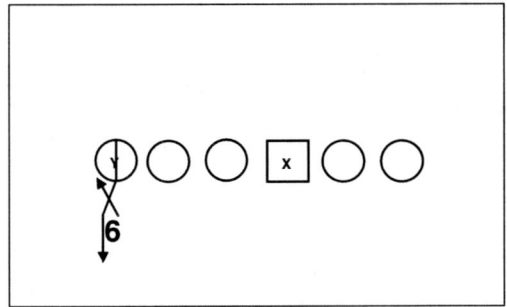

Figure 5-111. Outside release

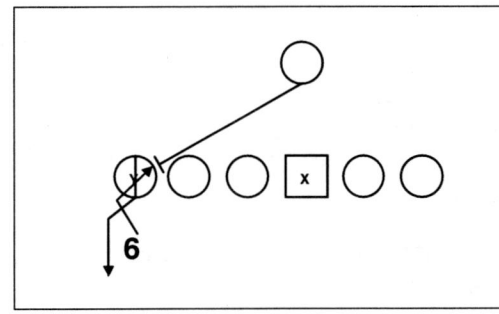

Figure 5-112. Near back kick out

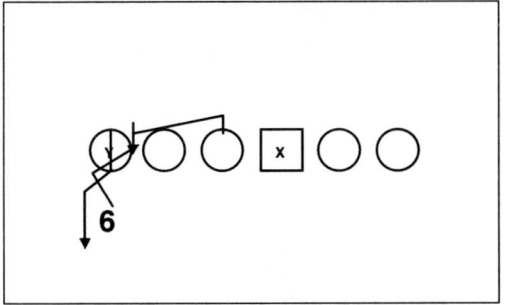

Figure 5-113. Guard kick out

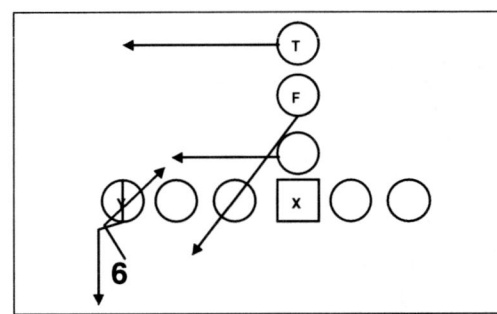

Figure 5-114. Option

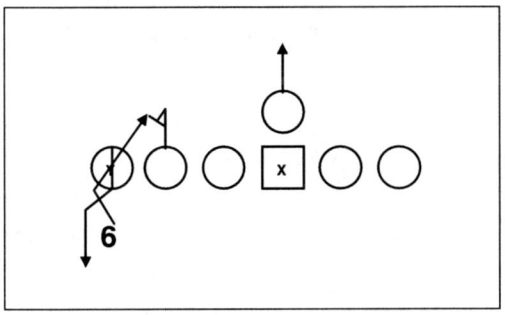

Figure 5-115. Pass

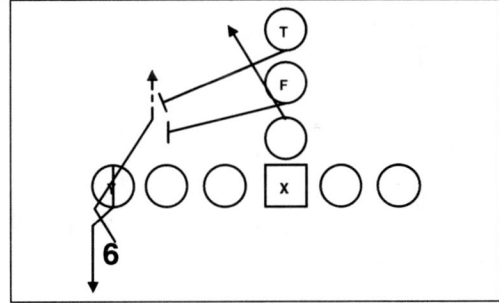

Figure 5-116. Sprint pass

7 Technique

Stance: Three-point

Alignment: Outside foot on the tight end's crotch (ability level)

Key: Tight end's hand, hat, and the ball (in his peripheral vision)

Execution: On any movement, attack the tight end

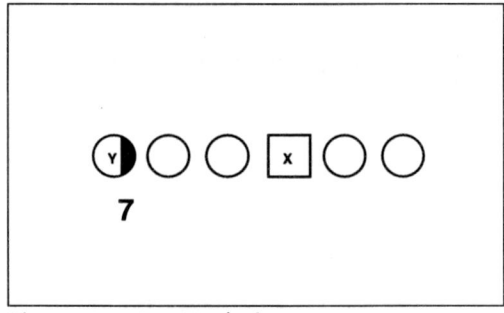
Figure 5-117. 7 technique

Responsibility:
- Run to: C gap
- Run away: Chase
- Pass: Cage

Types of Blocks

Base (Figure 5-118): The number one block to defeat. The 7 technique attacks the inside shoulder of the end and powers him upfield. The defender must hold the point. He mustn't run around the block, but instead fight pressure. Use steer technique. The defender pushes with his outside hand on the pec and pulls with the inside hand on the cuff.

Shoeshine (Figure 5-119): Play this block from the ground up. The 7 technique must keep the end off of his legs. The end will seek to place his outside ear on the 7 technique's inside leg. The defender must flatten the end's head and try to turn the end's shoulders perpendicular to the line of scrimmage. The 7 technique   still has chase responsibilities.

Figure 5-118. Base

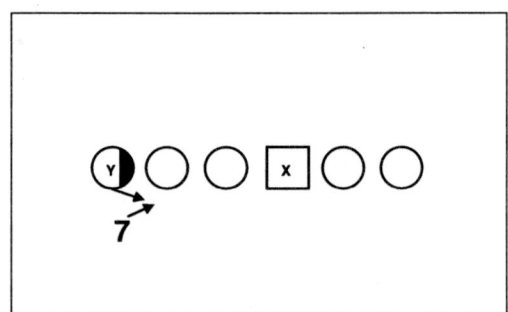
Figure 5-119. Shoeshine

Outside Release (Figure 5-120): The 7 technique will get back inside quickly off the six-inch attack step. He will read the block of the tackle. If the tackle reaches, press him upfield. Spill any inside-out blocks.

Pass (Figure 5-121): The 7 technique must read high hats and gain ground quickly. He will rush C gap. The 7 technique has cage on the quarterback.

Down (Figure 5-122): The 7 technique will attack the V of the neck keeping the inside leverage. He must not allow the tackle to cross his face. *This block should never be allowed to happen.*

Double (Figure 5-123): Drive the end into the backfield. The tackle will be negated if the blockers are forced to different levels.

Scoop (Figure 5-124): The 7 technique must not be driven off the line of scrimmage, nor allow the tackle a free release to the second level. If the defender can grab the slip blocker (tackle) with his playside hand, it would serve to keep the tackle off the linebacker and propel the defender away from the offensive end. The 7 technique should stay low and work to stay in the crease keeping his playside arm and leg free.

Zone (Figure 5-125): The offensive end may outside release, or rub to the second level. If the end outside releases, the 7 technique must get his eyes inside on the tackle. If the tackle is attacking with a flat head, push off him with hands and pursue down the line of scrimmage. If the end seeks to chip or rub, treat it as a base or double-

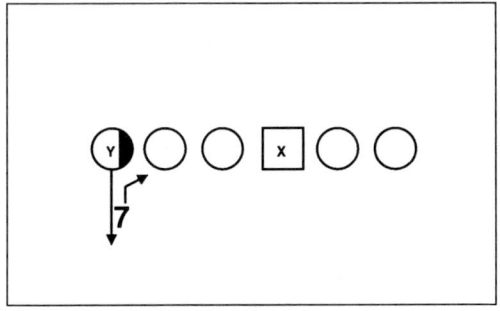

Figure 5-120. Outside release

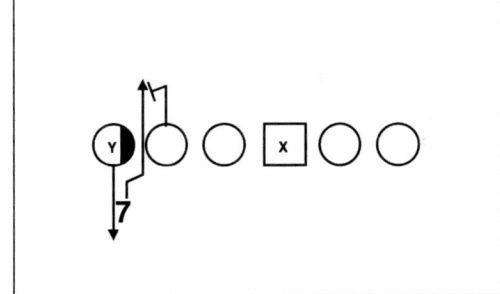

Figure 5-121. Pass

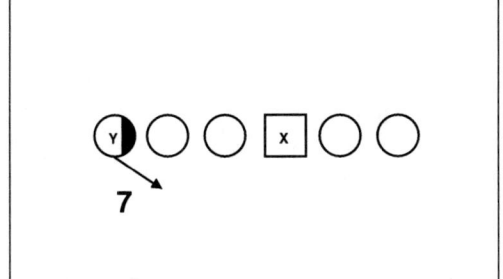

Figure 5-122. Down

Figure 5-123. Double

team. Take the fight to the end. As the 7 technique feels the end leaving he must fight to keep his head in the crack. He should throw his hips outside.

End Pulling With the Tackle Angle Blocking (Figure 5-126): This inside fold or Ed block consists of the end pulling inside and the tackle angle blocking. When the end pulls inside, the defender should take his eyes to the tackle. If the tackle's head is behind the 7 technique's hip, he can backdoor or half moon the tackle staying close to the tackle's heels (Figure 5-127). If the tackle's head is in front of the 7 technique he can crossface the blocker (Figure 5-128). If the tackle's head is in the correct spot, the defender should treat this as a base block and squeeze the adjacent gap with the tackle's body.

Figure 5-124. Scoop

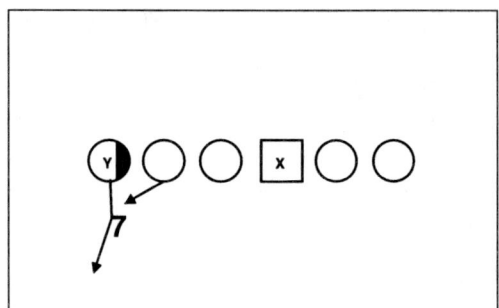

Figure 5-125. Zone

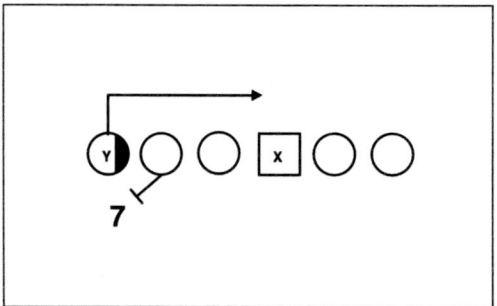

Figure 5-126. End pulling with the tackle angle blocking

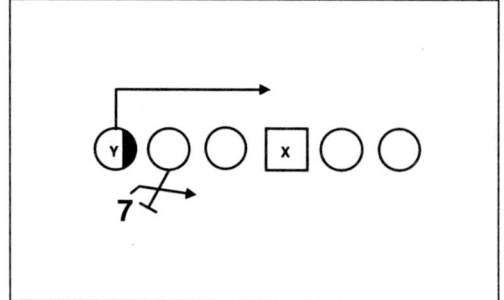

Figure 5-127. Half moon

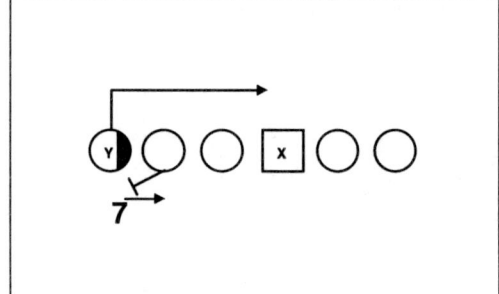

Figure 5-128. Crossface

9 Technique

Stance: Three-point

Alignment: Place inside foot on the tight end's crotch (ability level)

Key: Tight end's hand, hat, and the ball (in his peripheral vision)

Execution: On any movement attack the tight end

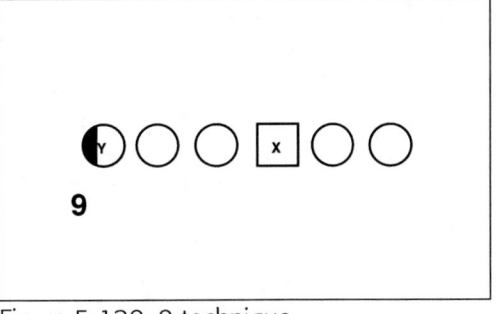

Figure 5-129. 9 technique

Responsibility:
- Run to: D gap
- Run away: C gap
- Pass: Cage

Types of Blocks

Base (Figure 5-130): The number one block to defeat. Attack the V of the tight end's neck, claw the blocker. The 9 technique should power the tight end upfield while leveraging D gap. He must maintain D gap by fighting pressure. He uses the steer technique by pressing the blocker's outside pec with the inside hand and pulling the cuff area with the outside hand. He shouldn't open up C gap by running upfield. He must play the block outside-in. Versus a high wall block, the 9 technique should squeeze and check for bootleg, cutback, and reverse (BCR). He will get as deep as the ball in case it comes back to him.

Down (Figure 5-131): The 9 technique should attack the V of the neck. The 9 technique will squeeze and replace the end. He will get his outside hand on the end's hip or base of the numbers. He will think dive to pull lane. He should spill any inside-out blocks.

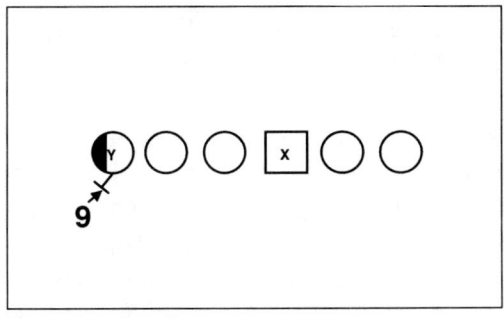

Figure 5-130. Base

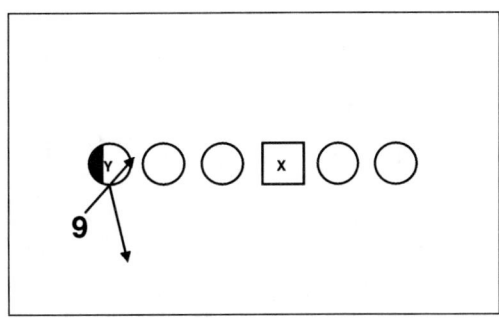

Figure 5-131. Down

Reach (Figure 5-132): The 9 technique should attack the end's outside shoulder using his hands and locking out. He will turn the blocker's shoulders toward the sideline using a long arm/short arm technique (steer technique). He is coached to work to the spot (4x1), driving the end upfield. Set the point. An important key is to attack the man when the ball is snapped. Beat him to the punch. Another key for the 9 technique is to keep his hips outside. Versus a jump-reach, the defender should regain initial positioning without committing outside too quickly. He should force the end upfield and anticipate falling back inside should the ball cut back.

Cut Reach: If the blocker drives his head below the knee level of the defender, the defender should drive the blocker's head down and away. Giving a little ground is permissible to keep the outside leg free. The defender cannot allow the end to leverage his outside leg. The ground should be made up, however, as quickly as possible.

Outside Release (Figure 5-133): The 9 technique should respect the initial angle of the end. Early on it looks like a reach. The 9 technique should ride the end with his hands and get his eyes inside when he realizes the end is releasing. The 9 technique should locate the next blocking threat. He should look first to the pull lane then to nearest back. Possibilities off an outside release include:

- Near Back Kick Out (Figure 5-134): When the 9 technique recognizes the back is on an inside-out angle, he should disengage the end, drive off his outside foot and attack the back using a wrong arm or spill technique. He wants to bounce the play. He tries to get his head in C gap. Spill the play.
- Guard Kick Out (Figure 5-135): The 9 technique should spill or wrong arm the guard's block forcing the ball to bounce. The 9 technique must get his head into C gap.
- Guard Pin (Figure 5-136): When the 9 technique reads the guard getting depth he should explode upfield and take the blocker on with hands while keeping his outside pad and leg free. The defender must force the quarterback to pull up and not allow him to stretch the perimeter.
- Option (Figure 5-137): When the 9 technique reads an outside release he takes his eyes to the pull lane. When he reads down the line action he closes and takes the first threat.
- Pass (Figure 5-138): When the defender's eyes get back inside to the pull lane he will see a pass set by the offensive tackle. The 9 technique will have cage on the quarterback.
- Sprint Pass (Figure 5-139): The offensive tackle will turn back or reach/punch and then turn back. The 9 technique must know the difference between a kick out or pin block by the onside back. A pin blocker will seek to leverage the defensive end's outside shoulder. The 9 technique must *feel* the fullback and *see* the tailback. He *must* protect his outside leg and outside pad. He should pull up the quarterback as quickly as possible and *never* allow him outside.

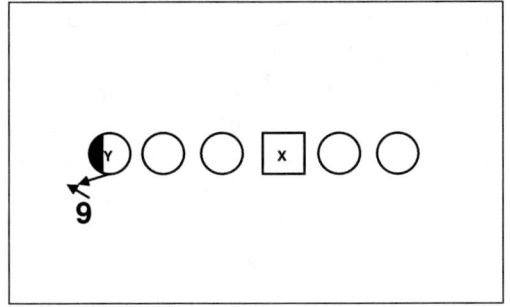

Figure 5-132. Reach

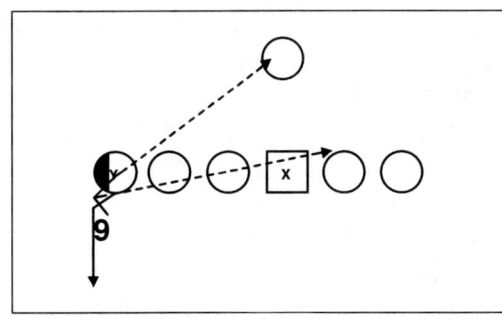

Figure 5-133. Outside release

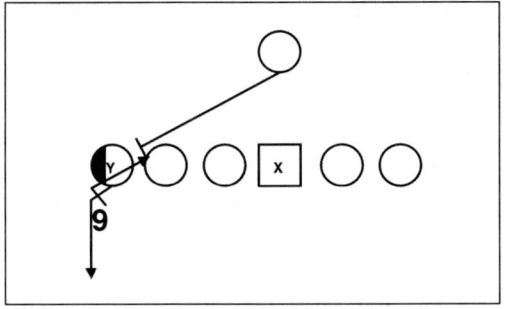

Figure 5-134. Near back kick out

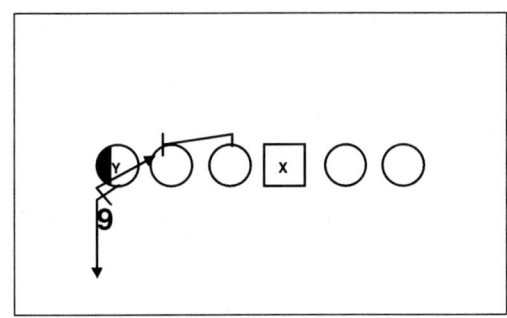

Figure 5-135. Guard kick out

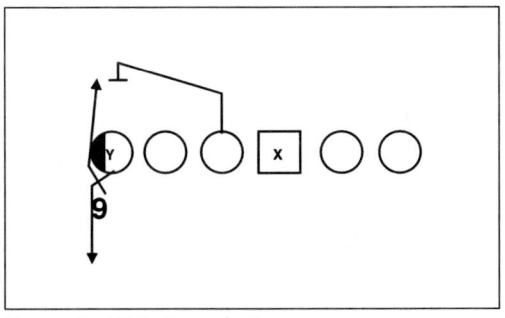

Figure 5-136. Guard pin

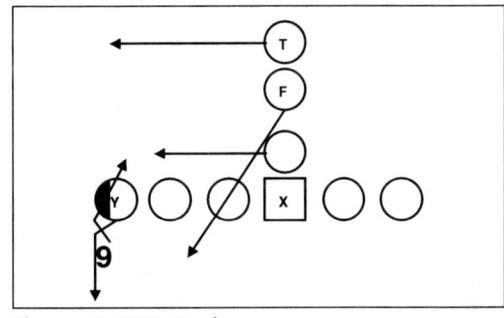

Figure 5-137. Option

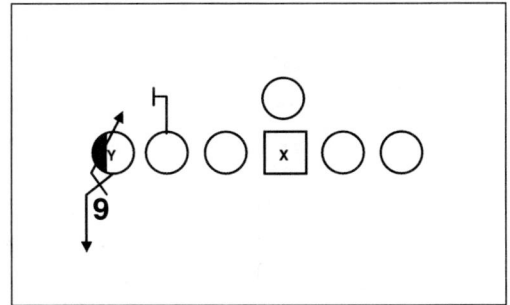

Figure 5-138. Pass

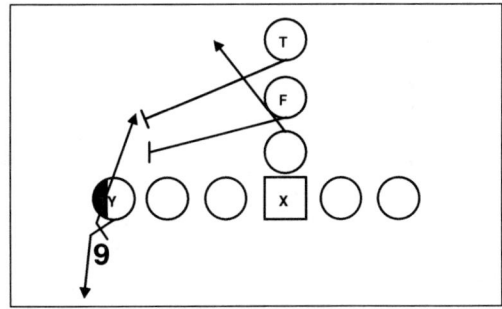

Figure 5-139. Sprint pass

Sprint Pass Off an Inside Release (Figure 5-140): A sprint pass off an inside release can cause the ends more problems than an outside release. A down block for a running play, or an inside release for a pass look the same to a 9 technique. On an inside release, the 9 technique must close and get his eyes to the pull lane. When no color shows in the pull lane, he must quickly get his eyes to the onside back. He must quickly discern that the onside back is threatening his outside shoulder. The 9 technique must explode upfield to take on the block. As always, on a sprint pass he must feel the first back (fullback) and see the second back (tailback). He must get the quarterback pulled up and not allow him to stretch the corner.

Cut-Off (Figure 5-141): The tight end's head will be in C gap. The block initially looks like a down block except the tight end will high wall the 9 technique. The 9 technique should squeeze the blocker and close C gap with the blocker's body. The 9 technique must not be knocked off the line. Be cognizant of bootleg. If the ball shows, get as deep as the ball.

Tight End Pulls Away (Figure 5-142): The defender must check the back for intentions. If the back seal blocks, he should spill it and chase. If the back slam releases, he must get width and depth checking for bootleg.

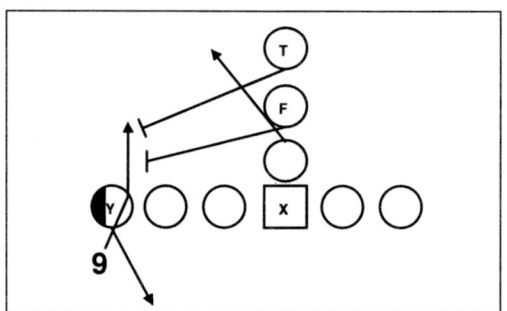

Figure 5-140. Sprint pass off an inside release

Figure 5-141. Cut-off

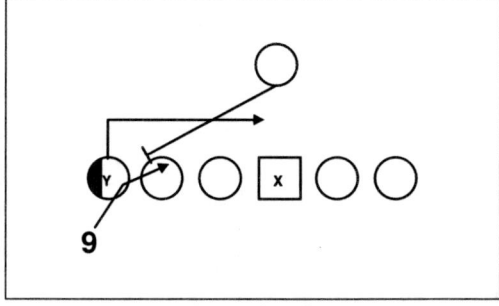

Figure 5-142. Tight end pulls away

6

Pass Rush

Attitude

As in any endeavor, attitude is crucial. To be successful as a defensive team—and more specifically as a pass rush unit—the correct attitude must be nurtured and enrooted in each defensive lineman. You, as the coach, must define success. If players think the only definition of success is a sack, you are going to have a lot of disappointed players.

Players must understand that success can mean many things. It can mean that the quarterback was flushed from the pocket, forced to throw the ball before he was ready, a tipped pass, a bad throw or a hit on the quarterback as he released the ball.

There are many ways to succeed in the pass rush. If this fact is communicated and understood, it can serve to motivate the defensive line and help to develop a winning attitude. A *great* pass rush starts with attitude. Each defensive lineman must have a burning desire to get to the quarterback. Different linemen will have different ways in which to get to the quarterback (i.e., different pass rush moves), but it all starts with the correct frame of mind.

Pass Coverage

Pass defense is truly a team effort. It is equal parts pass rush and pass coverage. A deficiency in one unit will adversely affect the other. Great pass coverage starts with a great pass rush. By the same token, a great pass rush starts with great coverage.

The pass rushers (defensive linemen) and pass defenders (linebackers/secondary) are interdependent. They need each other in order for their particular group to flourish. Each unit feeds off the other. To be successful in the secondary, there must be pressure on the quarterback by the defensive line so as not to allow him to wait for a receiver to come open. Conversely, the secondary can force the quarterback to hold the ball with good coverage allowing the rushers to get to him. Simply put, the better the rush, the better the coverage. And the better the coverage, the better the rush. A get-after-the-quarterback mentality is a good start in developing a good pass rush unit.

Effective Pass Rushing

Most novice fans think that unless the quarterback is sacked on a particular pass play, the pass rush was ineffective. Nothing could be farther from the truth. There are many positive results besides a sack that go unnoticed. Even though a sack is the ultimate objective of a pass rush, the following are worthy objectives also.

Objectives for Rushers

- Squeeze the quarterback's area. (Outside linemen should work to his outside shoulder. Contain an athletic quarterback.)
- Get in the line of sight of the quarterback.
- Don't allow the quarterback to go to a second or third receiver. (Don't allow him to hold the ball. Disrupt his rhythm.)
- Force him out of the launch point.
- Force the quarterback to throw on the run.
- Make the passer aware of the presence of rushers. (Cause him to lose confidence in the protection.)
- Cause the quarterback to fumble.
- Push or collapse the pocket to reduce the passer's ability to step up.
- Hit the quarterback. (Work him over.)
- Sack the quarterback. (This is the ultimate reward.)

Rushers don't even have to get to—or make contact with—the quarterback to make a contribution to an effective pass rush. A rusher simply getting his hands up is a benefit to the rush.

Benefits of Getting Hands Up

- Divert the quarterback's attention
- Bat the ball down
- Tip the ball for an interception
- Force a bad throw

- Force the passer to tuck the ball and run
- Force elevation of the pass
- Make the passer move his feet (which throws off timing of the pass)
- Obstruct the quarterback's vision

Even if the pass is delivered, there can be positive results for the defense if the defensive linemen disengage from the pass protectors and aggressively pursue the ball.

Benefits of Covering After the Ball Is Thrown

- Intimidate
- Knock the ball loose from the receiver
- Make big hits
- Gang-tackle
- Get in good position to block on an interception

As you can see, a successful pass rush has many definitions. Getting the quarterback to the ground with the ball in his hands is not always the measure of success in a pass rush.

Pass Rush Principles

As in any enterprise, certain principles or fundamentals must be adhered to in order to be successful. The following basic principles cover a wide range of fundamentals and coaching points.

Get-Off

Get-off, or takeoff, is probably the single most important element in pass rush. When the ball is snapped, the clock is running. Depending on the depth of the drop, the pass rusher has a finite amount of time before the ball is delivered. Normally, a rusher will have no more than three seconds. His mental clock should serve as a guide. A rusher does not have time for three or four moves.

Effective get-off starts with anticipation. Offensive stances and line splits offer clues to the type of play: light stances and tight splits usually spell pass. Recognizing the first thing that moves on the offensive side of the ball can help astute defenders beat the offensive line to the punch. In-depth scouting will reveal what moves first on the offensive side of the ball. It may be the quarterback's foot, butt, or hands, that moves first. Some quarterbacks will start their drop a split-second early by moving their dominant foot. Some quarterbacks will dip their tail a split-second early while others will flinch or open their hand under center a little before the snap. The author has used this last key with great success on a number of occasions. Alex Brown of the Florida Gators broke onto the national scene with five sacks in a 1999 game against the University of Tennessee because of this key on Tennessee quarterback Tee Martin's hands under center. What moves first?

Quick recognition at the snap will help speed up a defender's rush on his way to the quarterback. Does the offense present high or low hats? High hats usually telegraph pass intentions. Sound and thorough defensive game planning and scouting techniques will reveal passing tendencies by such variables as down and distance, field zone, personnel, score, and formation. A well-schooled defender has the advantage if he knows offensive tendencies. No matter the pass rush move of choice—whether it be a finesse or power move—get-off is crucial. The vital elements of get-off include the following:

- Close the distance
- No false steps
- No lateral moves
- All moves upfield
- Feet always gain ground
- Toes pointed toward the passer
- Get hands on the blocker (Don't make pass rush moves against air. Vince Lombardi said that hands and feet were 90 percent of the pass rush battle.)
- Low elevation (A low posture quickens the approach to the blocker and gives the rusher a leverage advantage.)
- Threaten blocker with speed to make him turn his shoulders (This way, the rusher can work the corner.)

Target

Pass rushers must know their prescribed rush lane and whether they may vary their rush lane. As a basic rule, the end's normal and most frequently used rush lane will be outside the offensive tackle. Depending upon the quarterback and game situation, the end can exploit the inside rush lane as well. However, the end must provide solid containment on blitzes unless he has a defender rushing outside him. The end's basic rule is to provide containment on the quarterback and make him step up into the push of the defensive tackles.

The rush lanes the defensive tackles use are much less restricted. The 3 technique will usually have the advantage of a two-way go on the offensive guard. Defensive tackles should strive to get a six-yard push. This push will keep the quarterback from stepping up to avoid the rush from the defensive ends.

If a blitz is called, the tackles should stay in their assigned rush lane. Freelancing may hinder the rush of a teammate or leave a gap unfilled. Defenders must know if they have the freedom of a two-way go or if they are part of a stunt that allows them to go under pass sets ("hot"). They should know how their individual rush fits into the defensive scheme for that particular play.

Pass rushers should know which pass blocker will block them and which shoulder or body part they have to attack. The defender must make the pass protector think he has to immediately defend a particular area. This is accomplished by defensive alignment and good takeoff. Speed scares a pass protector more than anything. Seek to force the blocker to turn his shoulder through the threat of speed, so the rusher can work the edge. Edge rushers are more effective than head-up defenders. The threat of speed in a particular area will cause some blockers to take the bend out of their knees and allow the rusher to exert and maintain leverage. The target must be conducive to a straight-line approach. The old adage that the shortest distance between two points is a straight line applies also to the game of football—especially pass rushing.

Pass Rush Planning

Effective pass rushers always have a plan in mind which they will execute at the target point. This plan is formulated through the study and influence of many variables. Film study of the opponent will reveal information as the defense considers what type of pass rush moves to use. It is important to identify which of the following types of players the opponent has:

- Short setter = takes on rushers on the line of scrimmage
- Deep setter = gets depth quickly
- Lunger = aggressive pass blocker

The following variables should be considered when formulating a pass rush plan.

Depth of the Quarterback's Drop

Pass rush moves must be compatible with the depth of the quarterback's drop. Not all pass rush moves are appropriate for all drops. Time eliminates some moves. With a three-step drop the ball comes out of the quarterback's hand in around 1 second or less. Pass rush moves should be limited to two-handed power moves. The best rush is probably a bull rush. Rip moves should be avoided because defenders will not be able to get their hands up. A typical throw from a five-step drop is delivered in 1.2 seconds, while a seven-step drop and throw takes about 1.5 seconds. Against a seven-step drop team, more elaborate pass rush moves can be used. Not all pass rush moves are effective against all drops. In addition, sprint action will eliminate many pass rush moves. Pass rush moves must be tailored to fit the opponent.

Depth of Pass Sets

Pass rush schemes must take into consideration the type and set of pass protection drops the offensive line uses. Pass rush schemes must be adapted to take advantage of how a pass protector sets. Defenders facing a soft set should use an early power rush while a hard set calls for a speed move or a move that makes the offensive lineman move his feet (speed rush). A blocker which tends to pass block with his head and shoulders down can be defeated with a quick swim. An offensive lineman who leans or steps forward can be beaten with a quick swim or run around. A deep set can be overcome with a bull rush and easily beaten inside. A blocker who tends to chase can be defeated with a foot fake. A good rule of thumb to use in formulating a pass rush scheme is to use power moves versus finesse schemes, and finesse moves against power schemes.

Summary

- Soft set = Power rushes
- Hard set = Speed moves
- Head and shoulders down = Swim
- Forward lean = Swim
- Deep set = Bull rush
- Chaser = Foot fake

One-on-One Match-Up

Defenders should also factor in other variables such as the one-on-one aspect. Some questions to be asked related to one-on-one confrontations include:
- What is the defensive lineman's strength/weakness?
- What is the offensive lineman's strength/weakness?
- What physical advantages does the defensive lineman have? (Is he stronger, quicker, or more agile than the blocker?)

Pass Rush Moves

An effective pass rusher will have in his tool box both initial and counter moves. Effective pass rushers must always have an answer in case the blocker stops his planned move. Without a counter move, the defender is defeated when an offensive man nullifies the original move. Defenders should understand and take the approach that when a blocker defeats a move he opens himself up in other areas. A rusher is blocked only if he stays blocked. Sacks can occur off a counter move as well as the initial move. A pass rusher who uses rip and swim moves as his primary moves doesn't have only two moves but, in reality, has four. If you include a rip-counter and a swim-counter, the rusher has four pass rush moves at his disposal.

Rip

A rip move is used when the offensive lineman's pressure point (shoulder) is up, or high, or when the rusher is shorter than the blocker. Rip moves should be avoided on aggressive pass sets, low shoulder pads, or when the blocker continues to retreat. The rip targets the edge of the blocker, especially the outside edge.

As the rusher steps, he should use an outside arm club or grab on the outside arm of the offensive lineman. The rusher seeks to push the blocker's jersey up and away from him. From there, he should drop his inside shoulder and violently rip his near arm through. He should finish the rip by punching himself in the ear. The rusher attempts to get the top of his shoulder pad underneath the armpit of the blocker. This allows the rusher to get his hips through and lift the blocker. The blocker is also lifted by the rusher rolling his hips. The defender should roll his trunk getting his eyes to the sky. If the blocker's outside arm catches high on the rusher, the rusher will execute a "pick" by lifting the blocker's arm with his outside arm as he rushes through. The defender's steps must be aimed at the quarterback. He must point his toes toward the quarterback. Once the rusher is even with the blocker, he should explode and run past him. A coaching point here is that the defensive lineman should stay close to the blocker's body and try to step on the *back* of the blocker's heel. Rushers should always remember that the right arm and right leg work together, and the left arm and leg work together. It does no good to get the arm through if the leg doesn't get through.

Counter Spin

This counter is used if the rusher feels pressure from the blocker's opposite hand (hand opposite the rip). If the rusher's hips are not able to get through, and the blocker is washing the rusher outside it would signal that the offensive lineman is overextended. The rusher should pivot off his inside leg and throw his outside arm and elbow inside with a 360-degree turn. Coaching points here would include reminding the defender to sit his weight down, throw the backside elbow into the blocker, and spin tight to the blocker using the blocker's body as a catapult to the quarterback.

Counter Swim

When the rusher feels the blocker clamp on the rip arm, he can immediately turn into the blocker and pull cloth with his outside hand while stepping aside. The combination of the offensive lineman's arm pressure, stepping aside, and pulling with the outside hand will cause the blocker to stumble or overextend forward. The rusher then should finish the move with an arm-over.

Swim

Swim moves are effective against blockers whose pressure point (shoulder) is down, or low, or if the rusher is taller and/or has longer limbs than the blocker. The rusher may use an outside club or elbow snap and then get the inside arm-over the shoulder pad of the blocker, or he may choose to pull the blocker's jersey down and toward him with his hand slightly behind the point of the shoulder while simultaneously bringing the inside arm over the top of the blocker in a circular motion. This circular motion is more of a stab just over the pad of the blocker, rather than an elongated clock-like movement. The rusher follows through with an elbow to the back of the offensive lineman and the hand should be extended to "spank the baby."

Once parallel to the blocker, the rusher explodes to the quarterback. As always, the right arm and leg work together, and the left arm and leg must work in conjunction. The arm-over must be thrown in the direction of the quarterback to get the hips and feet moving toward the passer. As always, the toes should be pointed toward the quarterback. The arm is thrown first with the hips and feet following. A swim move should not be used versus a high shoulder or if the blocker is still retreating. A swim move, as with most moves, is executed as the rusher makes contact with the blocker. A swim should never be made against air. All the protector has to do is stick the rusher in the ribs and the play is over.

Counter Rip

If the offensive lineman raises up as the arm starts over, the rusher can convert to a rip.

Power Rush

A power rush is a strong surge over a blocker or through either shoulder. The rusher attacks the blocker and tries to physically whip and overpower him and force him back to the quarterback—plant the "seed of power." Many times it is the best move for inside rushers. This particular move is good if the rusher is physically superior to the blocker or against a "rider." The power rush is effective against three- or five-step drop passing attacks or protectors who set soft or deep. Power rush moves should be used by everyone on the defensive line early in the game to send the protector a message. If it is used in the early stages of the contest the blocker will start to lean on the rusher. This lean will make him susceptible to a host of pass rush techniques. When offensive linemen brace or lean they stop moving their feet which is crucial to pass protection.

One of the keys to an effective power rush move is to get the hands inside by striking with the hard part of the hands (palms and heels). The rusher should lock-out his arms, which triggers the large muscles in the back. This lock-out, with a good low pad level, will force the blocker on his heels and elevate his shoulders. The rusher should have good bend in the knees, ankles, and hips. The rusher should use short, powerful, choppy steps. A power move is highly effective if used on a blocker whose pressure point (shoulder) is retreating. As with all pass rush moves, the defender must close the gap rapidly. Unless the defender is greatly superior to the blocker, he should avoid a power rush down the middle of the blocker.

Power Rush Keys

- Quick engagement of the blocker (Never *reach* for, but instead *punch*, the blocker.)
- Working the outside third of the blocker
- Hard, three-point contact to chest and chin (Contact with hard part of the hands and place the helmet under his chin. Try to get his helmet moving backward.)
- Establishing and maintaining a power position under his pads
- Maintaining key drive (Don't allow feet to stop.)

Counter Pull

If the blocker sets his feet and scotches, his weight will be forward. At this point, the offensive lineman will be overextended. When the defender feels the weight shift, he should use a pull and swim move using the blocker's momentum to accelerate to the quarterback.

Hip Flip

This move can be used as a counter off the power move, or as a primary pass rush move off the *threat* of a power rush move. As was stated earlier, power rush moves can be used to set up other moves. The hip flip is an example. If it is to be used as a primary move, the rusher attacks the blocker with quick explosive three-point contact which causes the blocker to brace or lean forward in anticipation of another power rush. However, at the point of contact the rusher will immediately pull the blocker's shoulders down and inside, and at the same time flip his hips to the inside and upfield. At this point the rusher's hip and shoulders are perpendicular to the line of scrimmage. As the hips get outside, the rusher will use a rip or swim depending upon the elevation of the blocker's shoulders. A low shoulder profile by the blocker will necessitate a swim, whereas a high shoulder will call for a rip.

Speed Rush

This technique is used chiefly by outside edge alignments, especially defensive ends or outside linebackers. This particular move is designed to outrun blockers who set inside too much, have slow footwork, or cross over to engage rushers. A prime objective is to sprint to a point one shoulder wider to defeat a blocker's poor footwork or a deficiency in quickness. A speed rush is best used by a wide alignment with a slightly pointed in stance which facilitates a direct line to the quarterback's launch point. This launch point can change from opponent to opponent. It is also used as a drive directly upfield to avoid immediate contact.

The rusher strives to stay on the edge of the blocker. Horizontal width is required to get offensive linemen on an island, removed from teammates. The basic offensive tackle set line is from his alignment to a spot four yards off the line of scrimmage and at an angle of 70 degrees and straight back four more yards. Speed rushers should seek to beat the tackle to this spot (spot of engagement). In doing so, the rusher will force the offensive lineman out of his kick step/slide footwork. If the rusher beats him to the spot, he should rip and "run the hoop." Should the blocker abandon his kick slide technique early, he will be susceptible to an inside counter move. The defensive end should always plant the "seed of speed."

Not only is horizontal alignment critical, vertical alignment is also decisive. Speed rusher should have a credit card alignment in relationship to the line of scrimmage. They should squeeze the line of scrimmage as much as possible. A key to the success of a speed rush is to close the distance as quickly as possible. This is best done by crowding the line of scrimmage. Care must be taken, however, that defenders don't line up on a man because offensive linemen will back off the ball as much as legally possible to gain separation on the rushers. Defenders must line up on the ball.

On the snap, rushers will explode off the ball. On all speed rushes, for explosion and speed, the defender must be sure all cleats are in the ground for traction. The defender tries to beat the blocker out of his stance. The rusher aims for a spot four yards behind the blocker and tries to outrun him for that four yard stretch. Beating the blocker to the spot will cause the blocker to turn his shoulders away from the line of scrimmage. The rusher tries to grab the blocker's outside shoulder with his outside hand and pulls himself into the blocker while leaning into the blocker and dipping his inside shoulder into the blocker with an uppercut. The rusher should stay low and press the blocker. The defender must keep a path or angle as tight to the blocker as possible. He should accelerate and sharpen the angle to the passer. The rusher should point his toes to the quarterback, and as the quarterback steps up the rusher should reach for him with his outside hand.

Speed Rush Principles

- Try to beat the blocker out of his stance.
- Aim for a point four yards behind the blocker (try to beat him there).
- Get the blocker's shoulders turned by the threat of speed.
- Use an elongated first step.
- Grab cloth.
- Break down the blocker.
- Get to the corner and run.
- Use a low pad level.

Counter Club

This counter is used when the blocker's head is upfield as far as the rusher's outside shoulder. At this point, the rusher should club or pull with his inside arm on the blocker's inside half. With the blocker's weight outside, the rusher can rip or swim back inside. A spin can also be used.

Inside Counter

This particular move can be used as a counter off the speed rush or as a move set up by the threat of an outside speed rush. As a counter it is similar to the counter club move just discussed. As a pass rush move in its own right it is executed against a blocker which overruns outside to the perceived outside speed rush. The key is the outside shoulder of the blocker. If the shoulder pops outside the rusher can club with his inside arm and dip inside. A spin off this club is also feasible. If the blocker's shoulder sets back the rusher executes a speed rush.

Foot Fakes

This pass rush move maneuver is based on stealth or finesse. The whole premise of the move is based on the threat of speed. If a blocker overreacts, or commits to a feint, he is susceptible to this move. In executing a foot fake, the rusher attacks the shoulder in the *opposite* direction he wishes to go. The rusher should give a good head and foot fake opposite the desired rush lane. When the offensive lineman sets to protect the threatened area, the rusher drives toward the target area and clubs the blocker's shoulder with the arm to the desired side. He should follow up by using a rip with the backside arm. The key to success is to get the offensive lineman moving in one direction and use the club to assist him in his weight shift to the threatened area.

Spin Rush

This pass rush technique can be used as a counter off previously described moves or as a primary move. The Indianapolis Colts are the masters of this particular move. This move can be used against offensive linemen whose weight distribution is overcommitted to one side. This move is especially beneficial to inside defenders who have a two-way go pass rush assignment. It should be cautiously used by defensive ends with contain responsibilities. If it is to be used, the end must not lose contain or have cover up responsibilities assigned to the defensive tackle. It is advisable that ends use this move only at the quarterback's depth. Of course, if the quarterback isn't respected as a runner, solid containment might not be so desired. This move also has value if the rusher is being washed past the quarterback.

The key to the spin move is to stay out of the middle of the blocker and work the edge. The genesis of this move is to sell the speed rush. When the blocker commits to the perceived outside speed threat, the rusher sits his weight down and throws his backside elbow into the blocker as he spins tight to the blocker using his body as a catapult to the quarterback. A crucial coaching point is to attack the blocker's outside shoulder with the rusher's spin side hand. For example, if the rusher is going to spin inside from a position on the left side he would attack the blocker's outside or right shoulder with his right hand. This would put the rusher in prime position to complete the spin to the defender's right.

Hump

The hump was popularized by Reggie White, one of the NFL's all-time sack leaders. This move requires above average upper body strength. The hump is set up by the rip move. The rusher explodes upfield, selling the speed rush move. The rusher will then club the outside half of the blocker, breaking down the blocker. The club is followed immediately with a rip move. This rip move attacks the outside half of the blocker's body. At this point, the blocker will lean into the rusher. When this happens, the rusher will slide his inside arm to the blocker's inside armpit. At this moment, the rusher pushes off his outside foot and uses the blocker's weight to throw him outside. The next stage is to explode with a hard inside move and get upfield quickly. This move is highly effective against blockers who overcommit to the outside. The hump is highly effective for defensive ends because of the availability of space on the edge.

Pass Rush Fundamentals

Following is a logical progression of pass rush fundamentals or tips through the various stages of a pass play from pre-snap to the sack or throw.
- Anticipate. (Know the pass tip-offs: field position, personnel, down and distance, score, line splits, and line stances.)
- Get off on the snap. (Don't be late. Keep pads low and numbers down.)
- Know the quarterback's depth.
- Get into proper rush lane as quickly as possible.
- Immediately recognize pass/run. (Recognize high hats or low hats. See the blocker's head pop-up. Is the play a pass or run?)
- Quickly and decisively make initial move. (one move/one counter)
- Keep momentum going toward the passer without lost motion. (feet and hands never stop)
- Close the critical area with speed and quickness. (Allow no separation.)
- Make moves at an arm's length, not versus air. (The blocker's only allies are distance and time.)

- Run in straight lines. (Keep feet, weight, and upper body going forward. Advance, don't dance. Keep toes pointed to the quarterback.)
- Make the offensive lineman move his feet. (Once he makes a stand, use his leverage against him. Push/pull, pull/turn.)
- See and feel the pressure point of the blocker (inside or outside shoulder depending upon which lane is to the attacked).
- Attack the quarterback's near shoulder in an effort to spill the quarterback (for A and B gap rushers), or attack the passer's upfield shoulder (for C and D gap rushers). (Make him step up into the inside rush.)
- Coordinate hands, feet, and head movements. (Use hard slaps.)
- Use your hands like razor blades, not sledgehammers. (Be quick. The hands are the quickest part of the body. Create unbalance by striking the blocker.)
- Keep shoulders in front of feet to prevent the blocker from getting under your pads. (Never show the numbers. Don't give up chest area.)
- Never be hat-to-hat. (Rusher's face mask should be under the opponent's mask.)
- Keep your eyes on the quarterback while your hands, head, and feet get you there.
- Turn the shoulders of the blocker and weaken his ability to stay strong. (Rushers can use speed, alignment, and technique to turn the shoulders of the blocker.)
- Seek to get hip-to-hip with the blocker. (Anytime the hips are even with the rusher's hips facing the quarterback, the only thing a blocker can do is hold.)
- Pressure half the man. (Don't work the middle. Working the middle turns into a strength tactic which takes time. Pressure is created on the edges.)
- Use the arms/legs together. (Right arm works with right leg—Left arm works with left leg.)
- Feel the lean of the blocker. (If he leans—pull. If he squats—push.)
- Accelerate when you beat the blocker.
- If blocked out of assigned rush lane, work back into the proper lane.
- Don't jump out of control to tip a pass. (Run through the quarterback. If a defender must jump, he should come back down on the spot he jumped from.)
- Stay on the quarterback's upfield shoulder. (Don't be worked past the quarterback. When being driven past the quarterback, use the blocker's momentum to crossface with a club, rip, or spin inside. A counter pass rush move or a power rush is automatic at the quarterback level. The worst place to be is behind the quarterback.)
- If the rusher hasn't reached the quarterback, he should get his hands up as the quarterback starts to throw.
- Execute a three-step change of direction (pursuit) when the ball is thrown. (This increases the chances for a big play on defense by causing a fumble, getting a big hit, or help block on an interception.)

Blocker Manipulation

To Move a Blocker Vertically

- Get to the blocker quickly as he seeks to establish a new line of scrimmage (take off).
- Don't try a move until the blocker is engaged. (Don't make moves against air.)
- Get hands on the blocker's pads, chest, and shoulder pads.
- Use hands to control the blocker.
- Lock-out elbows and knock blocker back.
- Keep face mask lower than the opponent's face mask.
- Turn the blocker perpendicular to the line of scrimmage. (Take away his squared-up position.)

To Move a Blocker Horizontally

- Create momentum in the opposite direction of your move. (Fakes move the blocker.)
- Use upper body for fakes. (Feet should always gain ground.)
- Deliver a blow. (Knock blocker off-balance.)
- Keep face mask lower than the blocker's face mask.

Screen and Draw

No exploration of pass rush technique would be complete unless screen and draw plays are discussed. These two types of plays are inherently tied in with the offense's pass game. As a matter of fact, the more dominant your pass rush is, the more likely you will see these offensive counter measures. It first must be said that a defender cannot be an effective pass rusher, *and* play screen or draw concurrently. However, that being said, you don't want a pass rusher who has blinders on and can't recognize screen or draw cues.

Screen

The guard and quarterback are good screen keys for the defensive tackle. The tackle and near back are good screen indicators for the defensive end. Screen plays, at their origin, appear to be just another pass play. However, at some point an astute defender will smell a rat. Some blockers will flash and leave, while others will drop abnormally deep and pull the rusher upfield. Still other blockers will pass set, and then cut the defensive lineman. The defender should play this block low to high. He should come out the way he went in. If a defender recognizes a back crossing his face or ducking inside, he should play down the line. If a rusher reads an offensive lineman leaving, he should jump in his footsteps or retrace if he has penetrated too far. If a rusher has gone too far, and is committed to the quarterback, he should continue and force an early throw. Some defenses assign a 1 technique or 2 technique to look for screen because they will usually be doubled or face a combo block on pass plays, which already seriously hampers their pass rush. If the blocker tries to cut the rusher, the rusher should plant and look outside. The defender should look for a receiver coming inside.

Screen Cues

- Abnormally deep set by the offensive line
- Abnormally deep drop by the quarterback
- Back crossing rusher's face
- Cut blocks by offensive linemen

Draw

Many draw schemes have the offensive line open up on the defender and flashing a lot of hands while keeping their inside foot on the line of scrimmage. This opening of the gate and overly-active hands should alert the defender to the possibility of a draw. The pass protector wants to invite the defender upfield, and then throw him farther upfield before he slips inside to block a linebacker.

When the pass rusher recognizes the draw he should squeeze the blocker by driving his inside hand to the inside jersey number and retracing his steps. Squeezing the blocker with the inside hand enables the defender to square up so he can compress the running lane. The running back will not expect a defender to come back from the outside edge. This gives the defender a good chance to strip the ball.

Draw Cues

- Offensive linemen have high hats
- Blocker's inside foot doesn't leave the line of scrimmage
- Blocker opens his hips parallel to the sideline
- Blocker tries to punch the defender upfield
- Pass protector has overly active hands

Line Pass Rush Games

The techniques described previously were tailored for one-on-one pass rushes to get to the quarterback. This section deals with pass rush schemes which seek to get multiple rushers to the quarterback.

Philosophy of Line Games

Line stunts or exchanges can be effective versus pass or run, and they prevent offensive linemen from getting comfortable by knowing what to expect. Generally speaking, having different stunts called on opposite sides is safer versus runs and more effective as a pass rush strategy than double calls. Line stunts may be called *quick* and executed on the snap or as a reaction to be used only if a pass develops *(delayed)*.

Quick stunts are especially effective if the offensive linemen get on different planes quickly, since this is an indicator of a man blocking scheme without switches. Quick games can force a man protection team to go to zone. If offensive linemen stay on the same plane, this usually indicates zone protection and slower twists may be more effective. Delay and grab games are desirable. This philosophy could force a zone team to go to man protection. Against teams that switch quickly, fake stunts may be called to cause switches on offense, which may confuse blockers once rushers return to their normal pass rush lanes.

Fundamentals and Techniques for Line Games

In two-man stunts the techniques are designated as a penetrator and a flasher. The penetrator is the rusher designated to go first. The penetrator always tries to get to the offensive man's back. His aiming point is a very important key. His charge cannot be punched and stopped, nor can it be punched and passed! If he cannot get penetration, he should recognize it, grab and pull the blocker who stopped the penetration in order to prevent a switch, and thereby free up the flasher. The rusher will actually block the offensive lineman with his hips, and if he has penetration, continue to rush with his feet, hips, and shoulders facing the quarterback. Anytime the penetrator is on an inside charge, he should keep his shoulders as square as possible to the line of scrimmage to keep from being washed inside.

The flasher always maintains eye contact with the offensive lineman. He must make him think that he is making a one-on-one pass rush move. He must recognize whenever the penetrator gets penetration, or gets inside/outside the blocker and then come around the butt of the penetrator with speed on a tight angle to the quarterback. He should turn up on the first sign of daylight. He must see the quarterback in case of a flush by the penetrator if he is assigned contain. Always run the game on the offensive side of the line of scrimmage. He must gain ground. Rushers should finish all games with a good pass rush technique.

Examples of Line Games

Pop (Figure 6-1): This lane exchange can be used strong or weak. It can also be executed to both sides at the same time. The tackle is the penetrator with the end on the loop. This is most effective against tackles who react to the outside and widen.

- Tackle: A speed rip by the inside rusher is usually effective unless the guard is too low. If this is the case the tackle should use a swim move. He blocks the tackle with his hips when they are even and he continues to the quarterback's up field shoulder. If the tackle is unable to get penetration he should grab and pull the OG to the outside. The tackle has contain on the quarterback.
- End: The end is the flasher and he should use speed to make the tackle get width which will give the penetrator a rush lane. The end will see the penetration and when he gets even with the hip of the tackle or beats the guard the end will come off the hip of the tackle tight and on a direct line to the quarterback.

Pick (Figure 6-2)

- End: The outside rusher (end) is the penetrator and must get hip-to-hip penetration on the outside hip of the guard. The end should stay as square as possible to the line of scrimmage to prevent being washed inside by the tackle. The rusher must keep his feet, hips, and shoulders facing the passer. The end should pick the guard with his body as he continues to rush the quarterback. If the end is unable to get penetration, he should grab the offensive tackle and pull him inside to prevent a switch-off.
- Tackle: He is the flasher. He should draw the guard's block which will buy time for the end. The tackle will then work outside. He has contain on the quarterback.

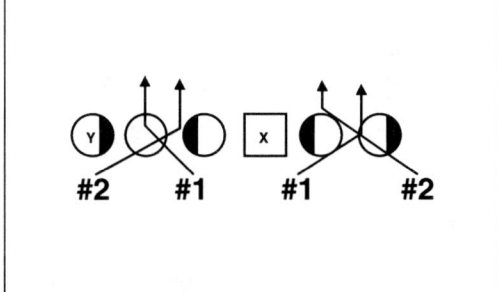

Figure 6-1. Pop

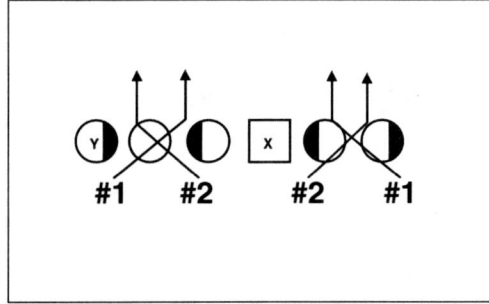

Figure 6-2. Pick

Delayed Pick (Figure 6-3): This stunt is the same as pick except it will be triggered off the defender's fourth step. A delayed stunt means it will be run only versus pass sets. Defenders play run first. Defenders want to sell a straight rush until they get to the fourth step. The end will give a "go" call to the tackle as he makes the inside move.

Delayed Pop (Figure 6-4): This stunt is similar to the delayed pick except the tackle will give the "Go" call.

Change (Figure 6-5): This stunt is a combination of pick and pop. The pick is executed to the open end, while the pop is run to the closed side.

Mixer (Figure 6-6): Mixer is a stunt where both inside defenders have contain on the *opposite* side of the ball.

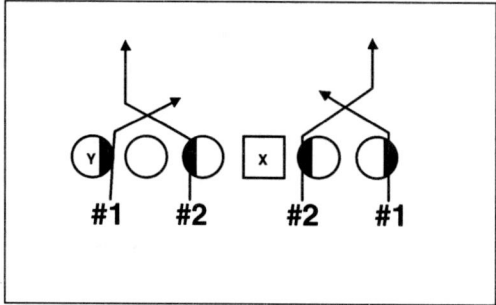

Figure 6-3. Delayed pick

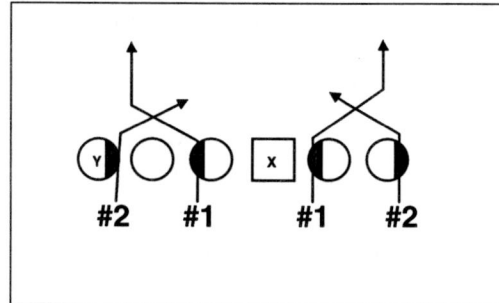

Figure 6-4. Delayed pop

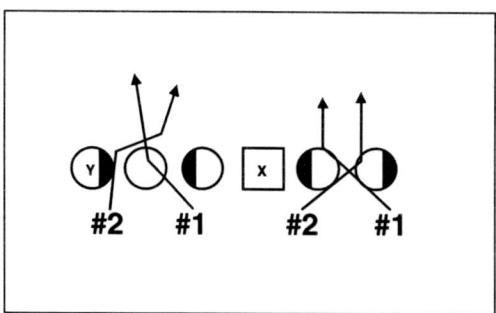

Figure 6-5. Change

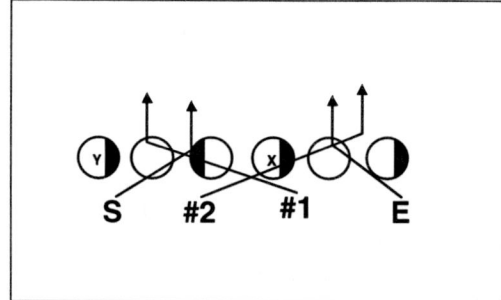

Figure 6-6. Mixer

Twist (Figure 6-7): The penetrator should ideally be to the backside (away from the center's blocks). The penetrator is the tackle while the nose is the flasher. The 3 technique works upfield two hard steps, plants off his second step, and rips across the guard's face. The tackle will attack the center's near hip. He will then work off the hip and explode to the quarterback. If the center turns toward the defensive tackle, the tackle will cross his face and rush the opposite A gap. The nose flashes at the same time the 3 technique attacks the center. At this point, the nose will loop tight to the opposite A gap turning up at the first sign of daylight. A read twist can be called which would involve both the tackle and nose reading the center. The defender that the center steps toward become the flasher. The defender away from where the center steps becomes the penetrator.

Cobra (Figure 6-8): Cobra is used in a definite passing situation. This call is used to get immediate penetration through the outside of the man aligned on. Defenders align as tight to the ball as possible. They will focus on the ball. On ball movement, the linemen explode with a hand slap on the offensive lineman's outside shoulder and do a hip flip. The defensive linemen must get their outside leg through while ripping or dipping the blocker's outside shoulder. From there the defenders work to the quarterback, keeping their toes pointed to the quarterback.

Cobra In (Figure 6-9): Only the two interior linemen execute the charge with both ends *mush* rushing the quarterback looking for draw or screen.

Cobra Out (Figure 6-10): This call has both ends on Cobra assignments with the tackles having draw/screen assignments.

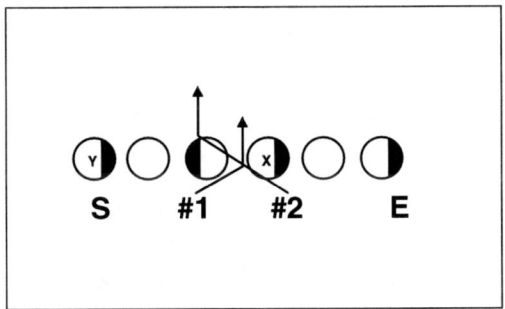

Figure 6-7. Twist

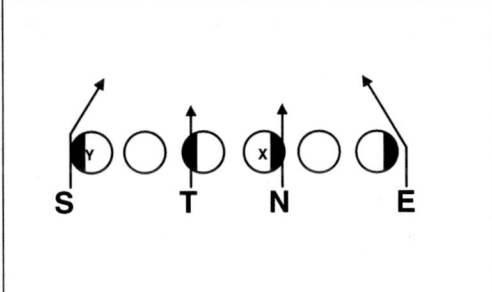

Figure 6-8. Cobra

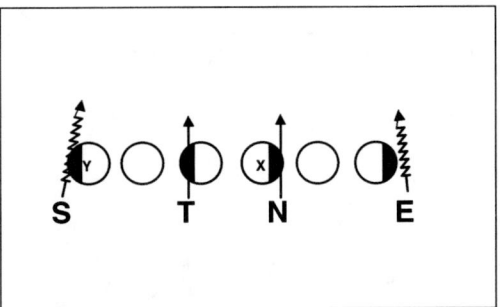

Figure 6-9. Cobra in

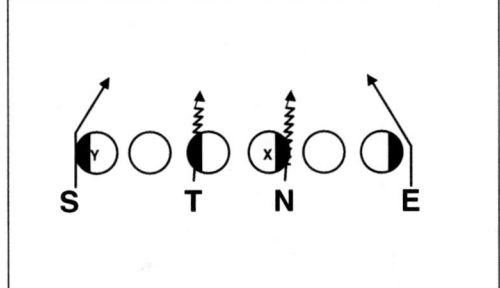

Figure 6-10. Cobra out

The following four pass rush games involve three defenders. You can use acronyms to name the stunts. The position tagged has contain on the side *opposite* the particular defensive linemen's alignment. Defenders opposite this lineman work one gap *toward* him. The remaining defender, who is aligned to the contain man's side, plays normal and will have contain to his aligned side.

Rin (Figures 6-11 and 6-12): Rin means "right inside."

Lin (Figures 6-13 and 6-14): Lin means "left inside."

Sin (Figures 6-15 and 6-16): Sin denotes that the strong inside man has contain.

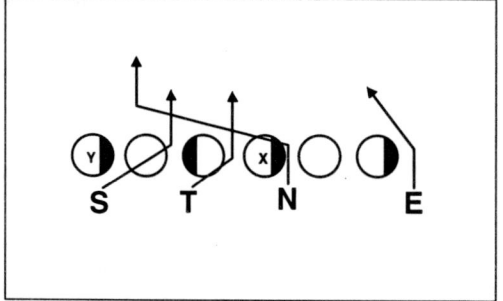

Figure 6-11. Rin—run to strongside

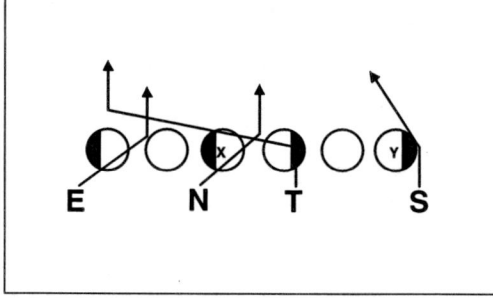

Figure 6-12. Rin—run to weakside

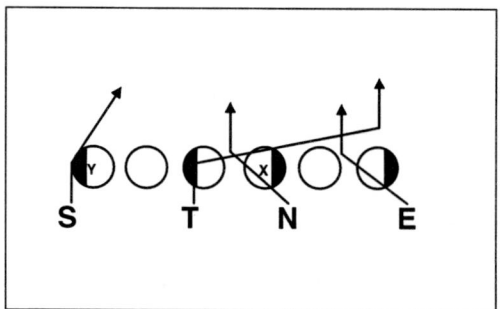

Figure 6-13. Lin—run to weakside

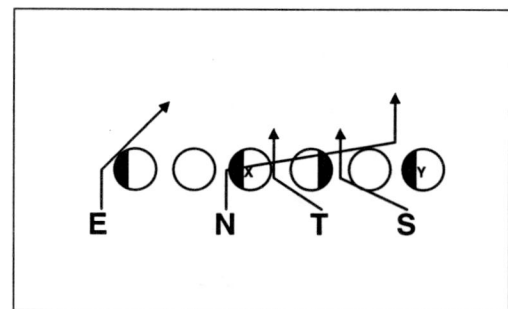

Figure 6-14. Lin—run to strongside

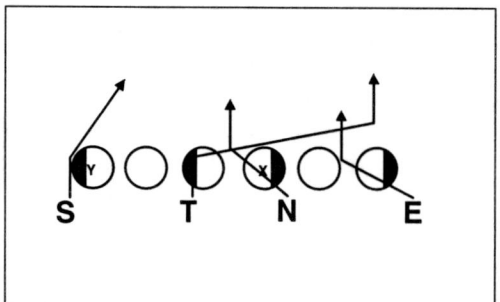

Figure 6-15. Sin—left strength call

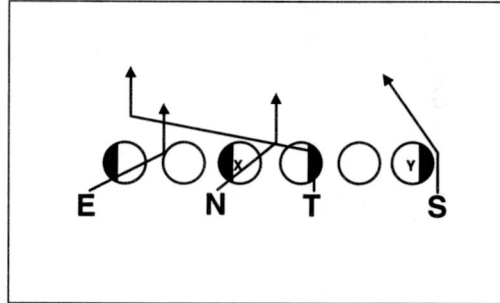

Figure 6-16. Sin—right strength call

Win (Figures 6-17 and 6-18): Win has the weak inside man on contain.

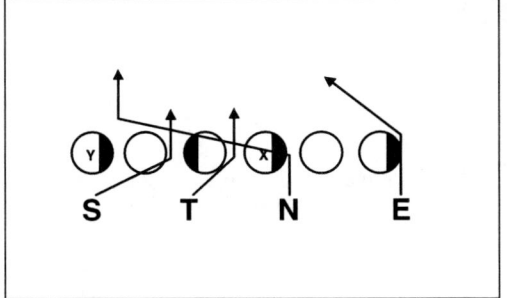

Figure 6-17. Win—left strength call

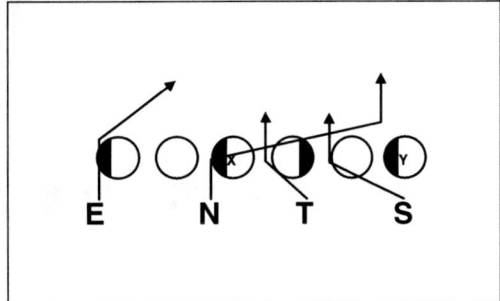

Figure 6-18. Win—right strength call

Green Front

The green front (Figure 6-19) has many inherent advantages as a tool to pressure the quarterback. Whenever green is called, defensive linemen get into a get-after-the-quarterback mindset. The previously mentioned pick, pop, and change stunts are excellent from this front. The read twist stunt is also a great change up in this front (Figures 6-20 & 6-21). The penetrator is the defensive tackle which gets the center's back on a pass set. The tackle to where the center turns is the flasher.

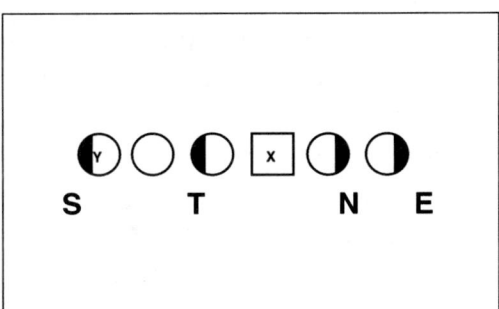

Figure 6-19. Green front

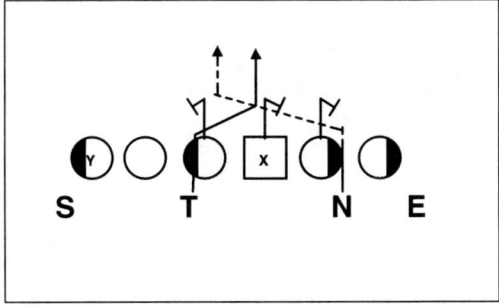

Figure 6-20. Read twist—tackle goes first

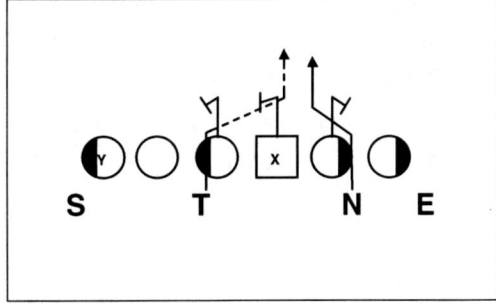

Figure 6-21. Read twist—nose goes first

7

Defensive Line Stunt Game

Many different aspects contribute to effective defensive line play. An effective stunt game is vital to a well-rounded defense. Stunts must be an integral part of any defensive line's game plan. An effective stunt game is needed for a myriad of reasons including:

- Stunts give the defense a chance if outmanned.
- Stunts give smaller/quicker players a chance.
- Stunts produce big plays (i.e., free runner at the quarterback, gets defenders at the handoff point, sacks, interceptions, forced passes).
- Stunts help defenses regain and hold momentum.
- Stunts help stop long drives.
- Stunts pressure both run and pass games.
- Stunts confuse blocking schemes.
- Stunts make offenses cut down or minimize play selection.
- Stunts negate some gadget plays and some slow developing plays.
- Stunts speed up slow players and make fast players faster.
- Stunts are fun to run.

Defensive line stunt principles include:
- Use the same basic stance and alignment as much as possible.
- Crowd the ball on most stunts.
- Get off on the snap. (What moves first?)
- Use exact footwork. (Step with the correct foot.)
- Take eyes to the man stunting toward.

Line Stunts

The stunts illustrated in this section are for defensive linemen. These stunts can be used as a line stunt only or in conjunction with linebackers or secondary players. Some diagrams have the line charge included in a coordinated stunt for illustrative purposes. This collection of line stunts is by no means all encompassing. However, it does illustrate the value of giving defensive linemen a three-way go.

Blast (Figure 7-1)

Blast is a 7 technique stunt. On the snap, the 7 technique works out to a 9 technique. He tries to get half a man outside the tight end. He is responsible for D gap. This is effective when teams are running outside and base blocking the 7 technique with the tight end.

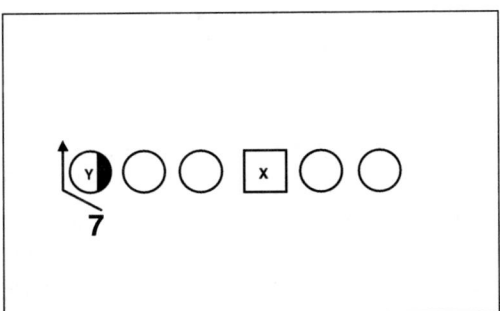

Figure 7-1. Blast

Spike (Figure 7-2)

Spike is a 3 technique stunt. On the snap, the 3 technique will parallel-step across the face of the guard. He will drive his backside arm up and through the guard. The key is not to try to cross the guard's face immediately. If the 3 technique insists on crossing the guard's face too soon, the guard could collapse or wash him down. If the guard blocks down, the 3 technique will work off his hip and replace the guard. Should the guard base, reach, or pass set, the 3 technique will work underneath him to A gap. If the guard pulls across the center, the 3 technique will use the fold technique on the center. Should the guard pull outside, the 3 technique must be ready to redirect. This stunt can be a combination stunt involving a linebacker or secondary player. Figure 7-3 is an illustration of a combo stunt (Mike spike).

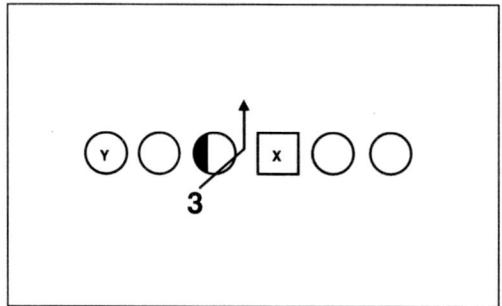

Figure 7-2. Spike   Figure 7-3. Mike spike

Eagle (Figure 7-4)

Eagle is a change-up by the 7 technique. Instead of anchoring C gap, the end will work at an angle to the fullback or tailback position. He can be coached to take whatever angle you want him to take. On the snap, the 7 technique will drive off his outside foot and rip with his outside shoulder and arm. His backside hand should touch the ground on the rip. This low rip will serve to protect him from a shoeshine block by the tight end. The 7 technique should anticipate a shoeshine each time he runs this stunt. The 7 technique still has contain on the quarterback should a pass develop. If the 7 technique beats the block by the tight end you have a free defender deep in the backfield.

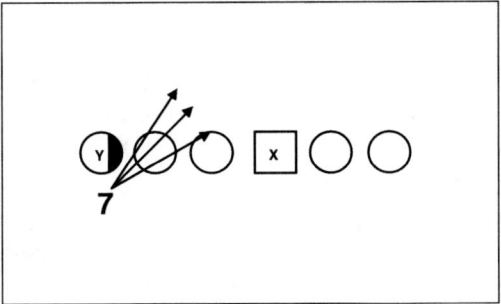

Figure 7-4. Eagle

End It (Figure 7-5)

This is a stunt by the defensive end. It can be run to both sides or to one side only. The end focuses on the ball. On ball movement, he attacks the V of the neck of the tackle. If the tackle blocks inside, the end continues on the angle and attacks the first thing that shows. Close all the way to the football. If the tackle blocks out or pass sets, the end goes under the block. He will spill all inside plays. He does not have contain. An end it—if run by a 7 technique—must anticipate a shoeshine by the tight end. The end must rip his outside arm low and hard to protect his backside knee. His weight should be on the instep of the outside foot. Like the tackle on the spike stunt, the end must not try to crossface the tackle. He must avoid being washed or collapsed. If the end goes through the V of the neck and the tackle blocks down, he will simply close and replace the tackle. This is a great stunt versus dive option teams. The ends will go under all other types of blocks (i.e., base, reach, pass set). Figure 7-6 shows end it in a short-yardage stunt package.

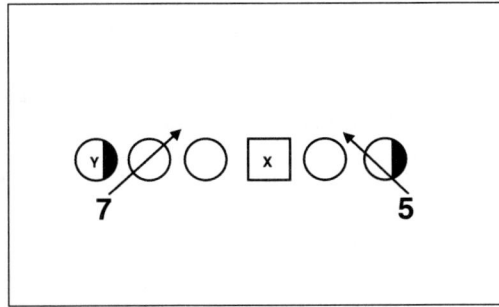

Figure 7-5. End it

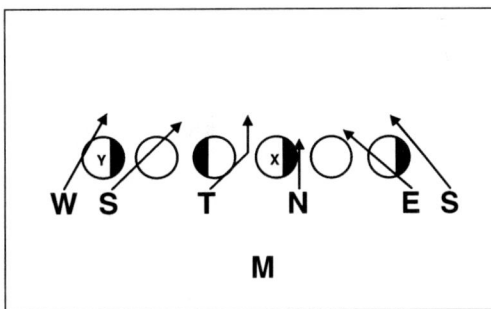

Figure 7-6. Storm

Jam (Figure 7-7)

Jam is an end stunt to the closed, or call, side. The same stunt run to the open end, or away from the call, is termed a taco. It is always run from a 5 technique. Unlike the end it or spike, the defender tries to crossface the offensive man. He will cheat his alignment but must be careful not to give the stunt away. This stunt can be used as a single defender game or as part of a coordinated stunt involving a linebacker or defensive back. Figure 7-8 shows a jam with an outside linebacker stunt. Figure 7-9 shows a coordinated stunt with the end on a jam stunt.

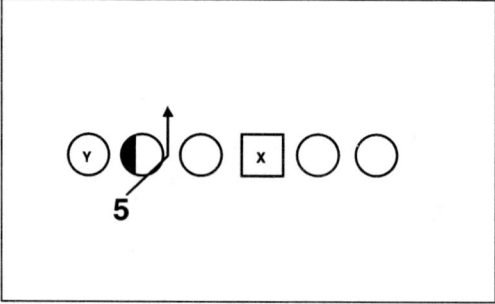

Figure 7-7. Jam

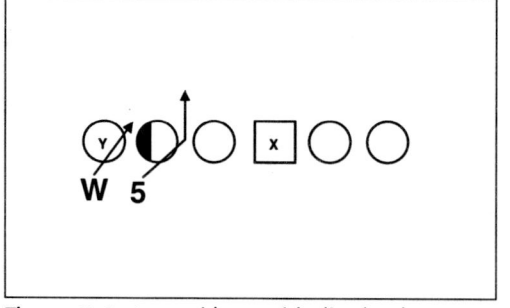

Figure 7-8. Jam with outside linebacker stunt

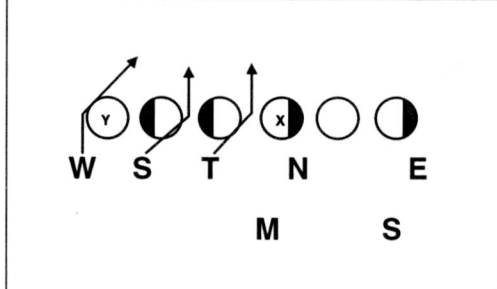

Figure 7-9. Jam with end stunt

Olay (Figure 7-10)

An olay can be a one-man change-up, or it can be a part of a much larger stunt. This stunt calls for the nose or 1 technique to crossface the center on the snap of the ball. The center can use one of two ways to cross the ball: he can step horizontally and rip his backside across the center's face, or he can try to grab the center's slantside shoulder and use it to help him pull across as he dips and rips his backside arm. Either move can be enhanced if the 1 technique can tighten his alignment horizontally, and loosen his vertical alignment without giving his intentions away. Figure 7-11 demonstrates an olay with a linebacker stunt.

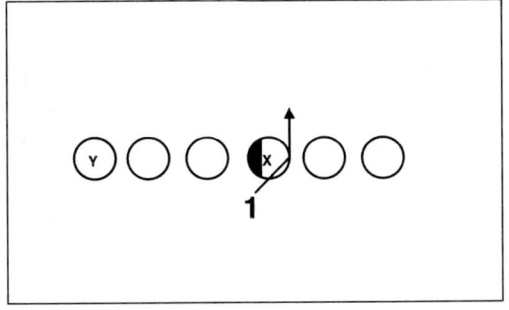

Figure 7-10. Olay

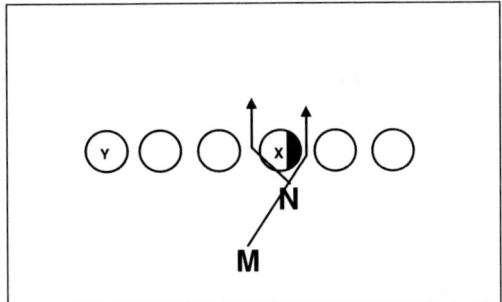

Figure 7-11. Olay with linebacker stunt

Pirate (Figure 7-12)

The pirate stunt is designed to stunt toward the bubble side of the defense. This stunt combines two previously mentioned stunts. The nose (3 technique) executes a spike while the end (5 technique) performs a jam or stick technique. The tackle can be schooled to work for quarterback contain if this stunt isn't supported by an outside blitzer. Figure 7-13 shows the tackle on a wrap around for contain. Figure 7-14 illustrates a pirate to the closed or call side. The nose will contain (wrap around) on a pass read if this stunt is run unsupported by a contain stunt.

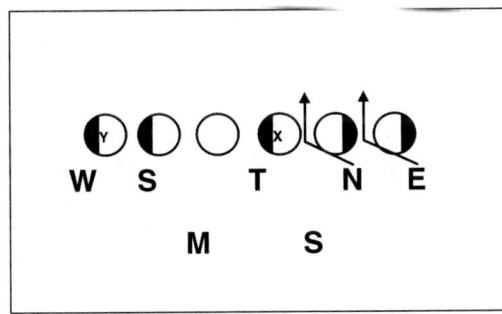

Figure 7-12. Pirate

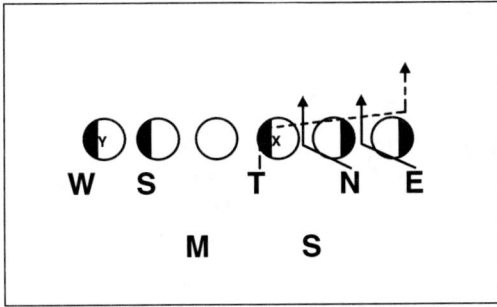

Figure 7-13. Tackle on a wrap around

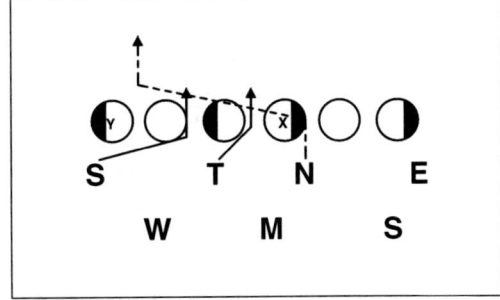

Figure 7-14. Pirate to closed side

Ricochet (Figure 7-15)

This is a 9 technique stunt. The 9 technique aligns in a tight shade and on the snap will crossface the tight end to C gap. He will not try to beat the tight end inside. On a down block, he will replace the tight end and on all other blocks (i.e., reach, base, pass set), he will go under. D gap is covered by a linebacker who is either on a stunt or scraping on key. The end has contain and chase responsibilities if there isn't an outside stunter.

Quick (Figure 7-16)

A quick is an inside charge by an inside shade. This stunt is run by a 2 technique. The defender will push off his outside foot while stepping with his inside foot. He must keep his chest over the knee while throwing his inside arm back, keeping the elbow tight to the body. The outside arm (covered arm) is dipped so he can skim the grass with his hand. This will offer the defender some measure of protection against a shoeshine block. The 2 technique should show the offensive man he lined up on his backside shoulder blade. The 2 technique should anticipate a shoeshine block each time he runs this stunt. He must not be cut off or shoeshined. Versus a tight split between the guard and center, the 2 technique should use a flat inside step followed by an inside-and-up action. The 2 technique should key the offensive man he is slanting toward (center).

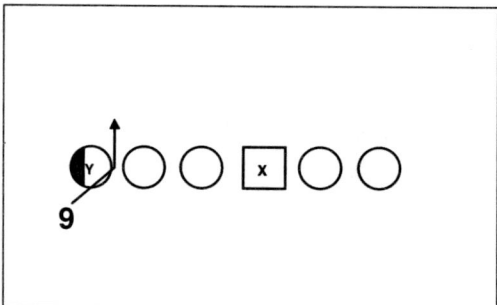

Figure 7-15. Ricochet

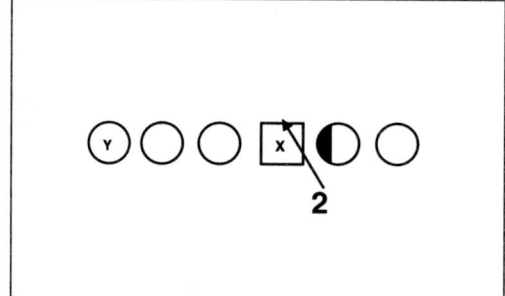

Figure 7-16. Quick

Tab (Figure 7-17)

A tab is a quick executed from a 4 technique. The mechanics of both the quick and tab are the same.

Taco (Figure 7-18)

The taco is a jam or stick executed to the open end, or away from the strength call.

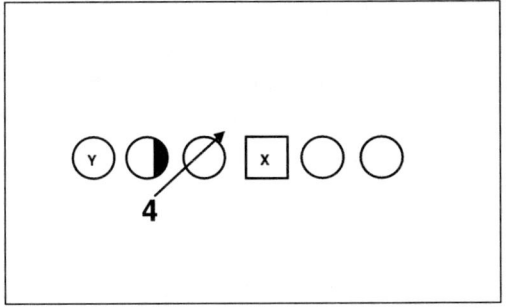

Figure 7-17. Tab

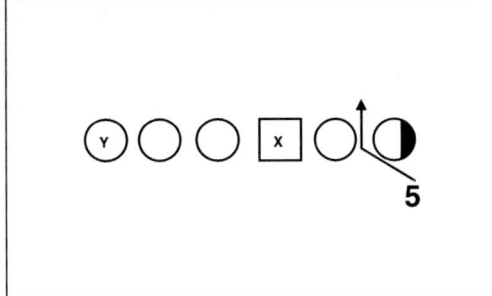

Figure 7-18. Taco

Slant Technique

Occasionally, defensive linemen will be asked to crossface offensive linemen while aligned in a shade opposite the slant. For example, a 4 technique may be asked to work to a 5 technique, or vice versa. A lineman can be called on to execute a slant from a 0 technique or head-up position, but for disguise purposes, it is better to slant from a shade.

To properly disguise a slant, it must be initiated from either an inside or outside shade. Linemen—when slanting—can cheat their alignment slightly, but they must not give away their intentions. Teams that play wide or loose shades will have a much tougher time of slanting than defenders who historically play a tighter shade. A tight shade lineman can disguise his movement more effectively.

Linemen, on a slant, can improve their chances by slightly backing off the ball and squaring up. This would serve to give the defensive lineman more room to clear. Defensive linemen, on a slant, should step flat with their slantside foot first followed by an up-step to penetrate the assigned gap. Slanters should try to get to the hip of the man they're slanting toward. Defenders should not look for the ball until they reach the target hip. Weight should be placed on the foot opposite the first step. For example, defenders slanting right should have their weight concentrated on the instep of their left foot.

As the defender steps flat to the line of scrimmage on his first step, he should rip his backside shoulder and arm through. This flat step keeps the defender from being washed down the line of scrimmage. If the man he's slanting toward blocks down, the slanter should close off his hip. He should, in essence, replace the blocker. The defender's toes on both steps should be pointed to the line of scrimmage. The defender's shoulder level throughout the move should stay the same as in the stance. The defensive lineman should eye the offensive lineman he is working toward.

Defensive Line Techniques

The following defensive line techniques are not stunts by definition but defensive reactions to offensive blocking schemes. To an opponent they might appear to be stunts.

Base Call

A base call in the huddle tells all outside shades (3, 5, 9 techniques) to play normal on all blocking schemes except a *base* block. Should an outside technique get a base block, he will go under the block and fill the inside gap with a linebacker scraping over the top. In essence, the defensive lineman and the linebacker have traded gaps. This is highly effective against teams which favor isolation-type plays. Figure 7-19 and Figure 7-20 illustrate weakside and strongside isolation plays and defensive reactions to each.

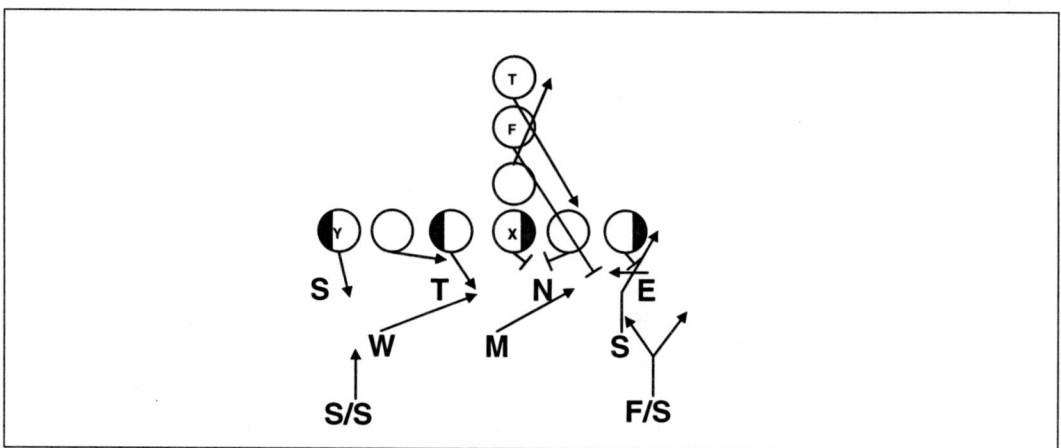

Figure 7-19. Weakside isolation

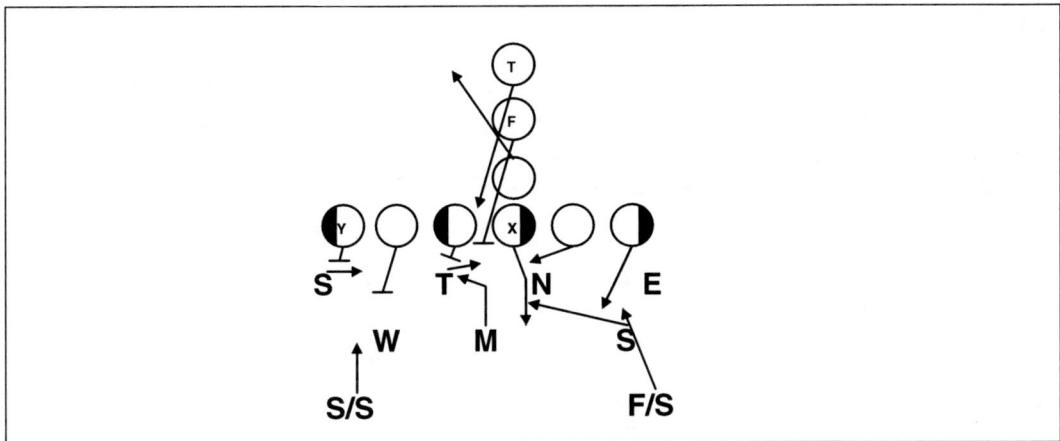

Figure 7-20. Strongside isolation

Hot Call

Anytime an outside blitzer gives a hot call, all defensive linemen who are in outside shades to the stuntside go under base blocks or pass sets. Obviously, inside shaded defenders are inside already. Figure 7-21 and Figure 7-22 illustrate hot calls. A hot defender has no contain or chase responsibilities. Those are assumed by the outside blitzer.

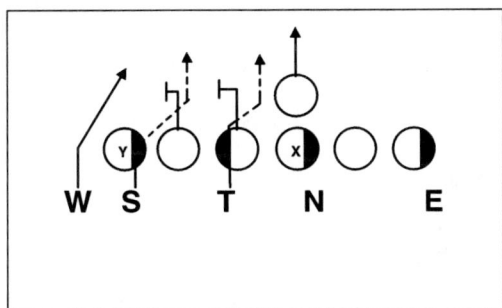

Figure 7-21. Hot call—strongside

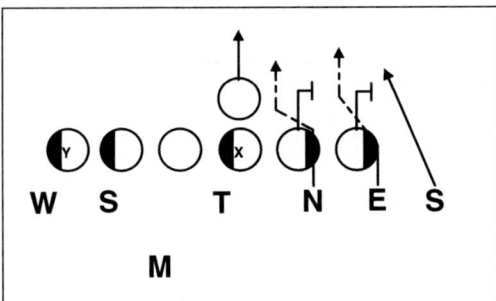

Figure 7-22. Hot call—weakside

Q Call

This is a change-up stunt by 3 technique and 5 technique defenders against option teams. These defenders will step down hard as if they're taking dive, but at the last second they will step hard upfield and take the quarterback. Figure 7-23 illustrates a Q call by a 5 technique end on a weakside dive. Figure 7-24 shows a 3 technique tackle on a Q call against a midline option play.

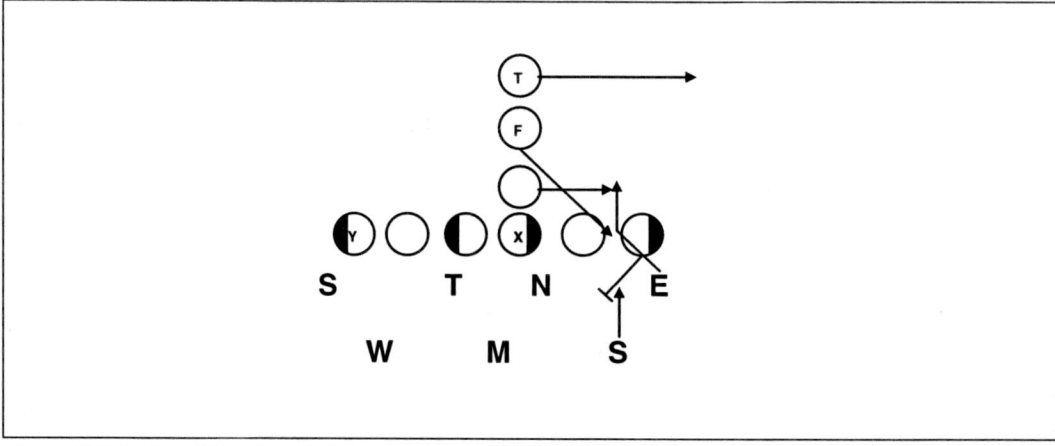

Figure 7-23. Q call by 5 technique

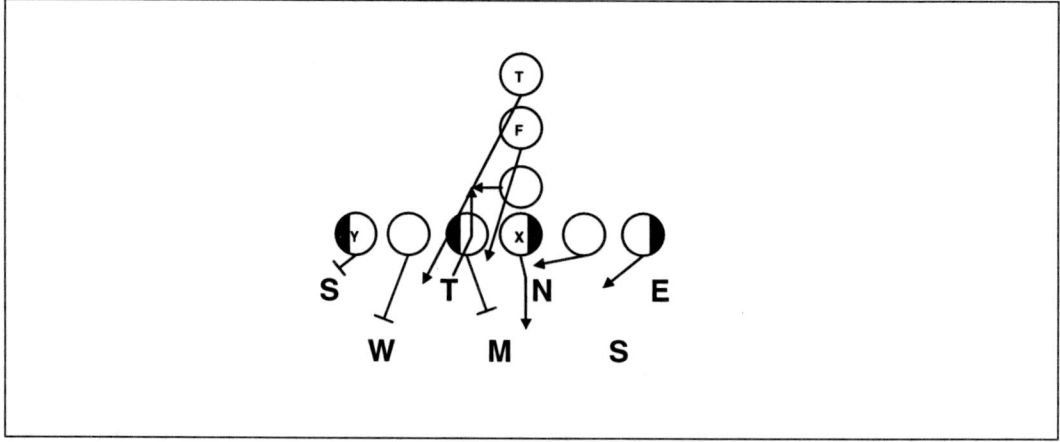

Figure 7-24. Q call by 3 technique

8

Line Zone Blitz Techniques

What started out in the NFL as a defensive wrinkle—the zone blitz—has now become a staple in all college and NFL defensive playbooks. Many high schools also run zone blitz pressures. Bill Arnsparger and Dick LeBeau are credited with giving birth to this novel scheme.

The zone blitz package allows defenses to pressure the quarterback and stay in a zone defense instead of exposing their secondary with man-to-man coverage. The zone blitz concept allows defenses to bring outside linebackers, inside linebackers, safeties, and/or cornerbacks with various combinations.

What is radically different from other blitz concepts is that in the zone blitz linemen drop into coverage to replace a stunting linebacker or secondary player. This movement causes offensive protection problems because a particular defensive lineman may rush or drop into a short zone to cover up for a blitzer. The basic scheme has a five-man pressure with a three-under, three-deep coverage scheme. In a 4-3 system, one of the underneath defenders is a defensive lineman. In 3-3 or 3-4 systems, a linebacker will drop.

Obviously, the lineman dropping in coverage—usually an end—must have some athletic ability. Even if only one lineman drops into coverage, the other three defensive linemen have important roles. Figure 8-1 is an example of a zone blitz.

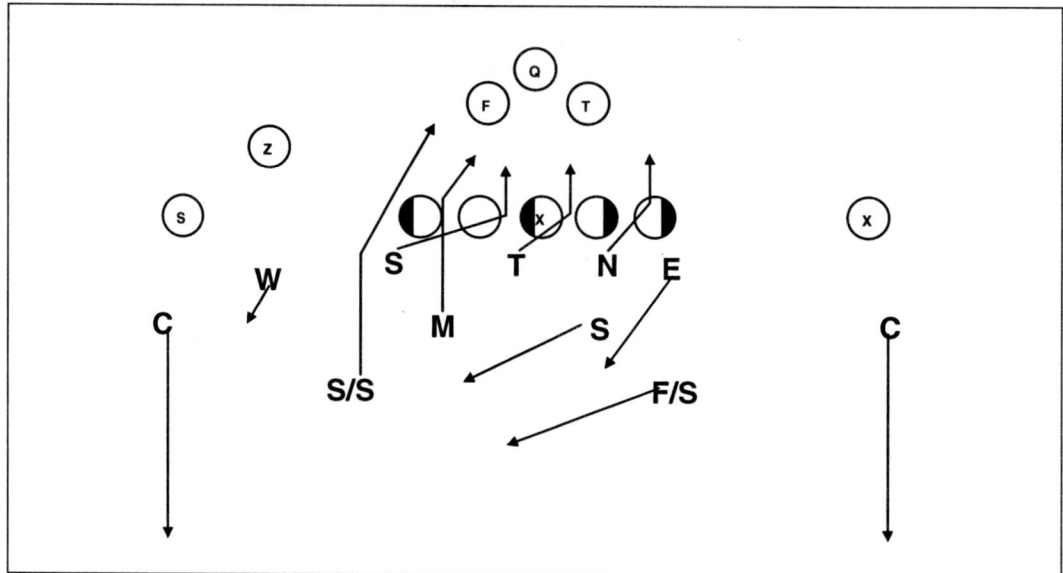

Figure 8-1. Under shark

This chapter will explore assignments and techniques for all linemen for this particular blitz. Though numerous combinations can be used to construct zone blitzes, the following are basic lineman techniques.

Assignments:

- Left end = Long stick
- Left tackle = Stick
- Right tackle = Stick to cage
- Right end = Deuce

Definition of Techniques

Long Stick

The end will slant two gaps. He works down to A gap. He should step with his inside foot while pushing off his outside foot. The end should rip his outside shoulder keeping a low profile. He must be strong and press upfield, and not be washed.

Stick

The left tackle will work one gap. He will cross the center's face to the opposite A gap.

Stick to Cage

The right tackle will attack the inside shoulder of the offensive tackle and work to contain the quarterback. Should the tackle work out or back, the defensive tackle will slip by and contain the quarterback. However, should the offensive tackle turn toward the defensive tackle, the defensive tackle will crossface the blocker to ensure contain.

Deuce

The right end is the dropper in this scheme. He will drop over the #2 receiver with outside leverage. If the #1 receiver is a tight end, the drop end will drop straight back while getting a hold up on the tight end. However, he should constantly be aware of any flat threat (Figure 8-2).

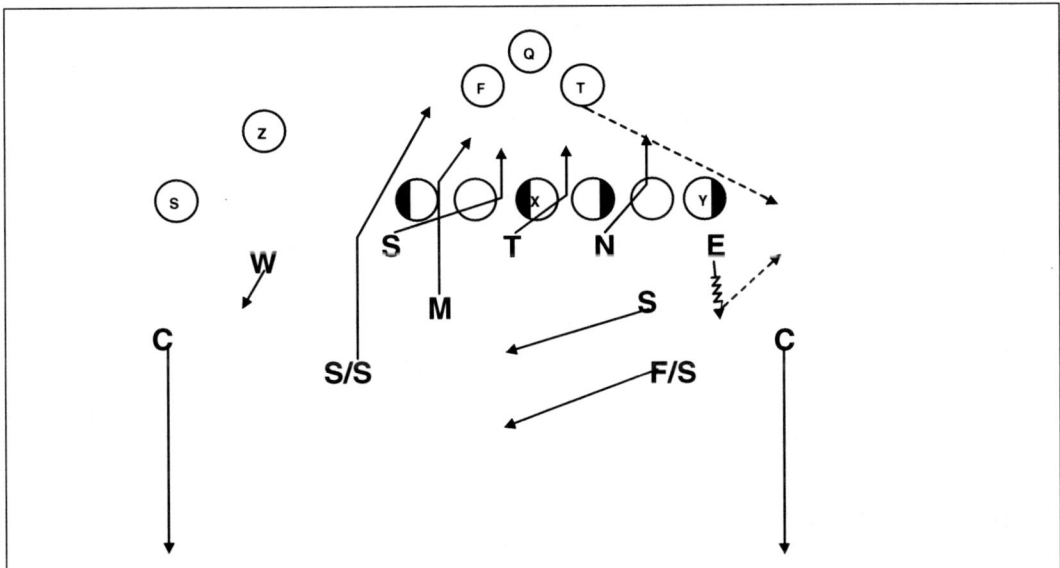

Figure 8-2. Drop end flat threat

Figure 8-3 shows under shark versus a doubles formation. Assignments are the same except the deuce end. Versus a doubles formation, Sam will assume deuce responsibilities and the end will assume Sam's assignment including a zone drop over the #3 receiver. Sam triggers this exchange with a "gut" call. "Gut" is a call used whenever there are two detached receivers to the drop end's side. With a "gut" call, the end will drop 10 yards deep over the #3 receiver.

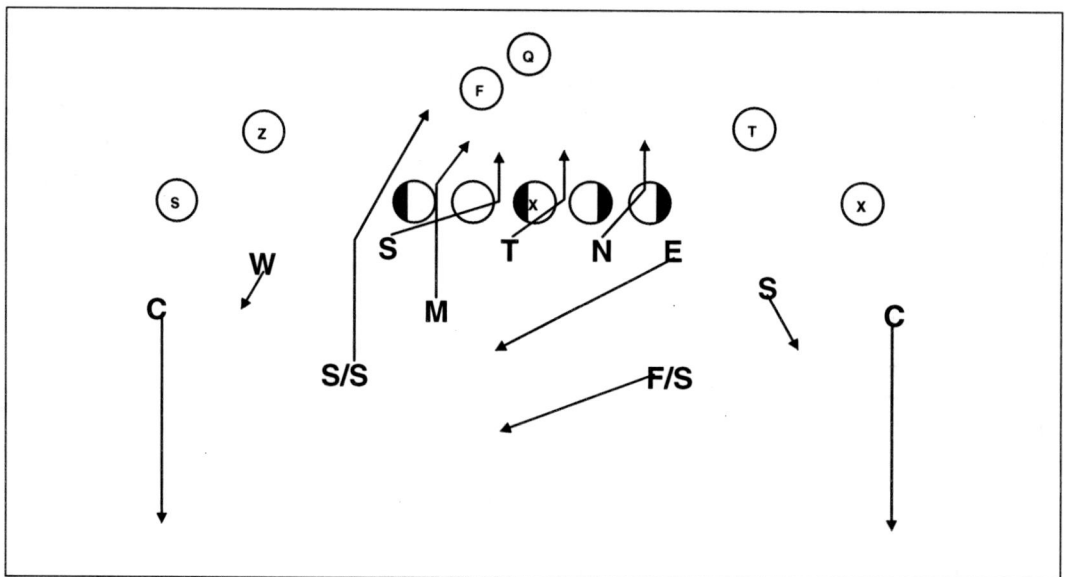

Figure 8-3. Under shark versus doubles formation

Deuce Coaching Points

- Listen for "gut" call from Sam. Look outside pre-snap. If you see more than one receiver you will get a "gut" call.
- Rule #1 is to never get beat to the flat by the #2 receiver.
- No tip-offs. Don't give stunt away by stance or alignment.
- Versus run, the deuce end has force. He must turn the ball inside. The end must be sure the play isn't a run before dropping.
- Versus screen, turn the ball inside.
- Fold on run away.

Gut Coaching Points

- Listen for "gut" call. Look outside. If you see more than one receiver you will get a "gut" call.
- If you receive a "gut" call, recognize where the #3 receiver is pre-snap. Count outside-in until you find the #3 receiver. The #3 receiver is the initial drop target. Drop 10 yards over the top of the #3 receiver.

9

Drills

Guidelines for Planning Drills

When planning drills for practice, ask yourself the following questions:

- How much practice time is available?
- What is the best use of the time available? (You may have to prioritize.)
- How should practices be divided into individual, group, and team periods?
- What skills are to be cultivated? (The cardinal rule of effective training is specificity.)
- Is the drill instructive or competitive? (Keep in mind that competitive drills, where the goal is to win, don't engender learning. As a matter of fact, some players may go into a survival mode in a competitive situation. Competitive combo and group drills especially can get out of hand. Therefore, competitive drills should be used judiciously, and should not be used in the formative stage of a new technique.)
- What tempo should the drill be performed at?
- Do service players understand their role?
- What attire is to be used? (Is the drill to be performed in full pads, shorts, or shells?)

Guidelines for Running Drills

- Choose drills that fit into the team's defensive system.
- Relate each drill to a game situation.
- Be precise with instructions and use established terminology.
- Follow the rudimentary teaching progression of *hear it, see it, do it.*
- Use sequence teaching. (Teach a skill in series. A systematic approach will build on previous learning.)
- Inform players what they will be doing in practice and why they will be doing it. (The purpose of the drill should be clear. Inform players the intensity level desired: walk-through, run-through, or game speed.)
- Demand a high standard of performance. (Be patient, but demanding.)
- Insist that players concentrate.
- Mix various types of practice to maximize learning and minimize physical fatigue.
- Periodically evaluate the effectiveness of the drills. (Do you see the taught skill on game film?)

The drills described in this chapter, although not all-inclusive, have been proven effective for teaching defensive line play. These drills are appropriate for any defensive system.

Agility Drills

These drills can be used to evaluate a player's agility, balance, foot speed, etc. These drills can be used as a warm-up or a conditioning drill. Agility drills can be done in shorts, shells, or full pads.

Inside Lead

Purpose: Teaches defensive linemen how to play over trash, on or near the line of scrimmage. It also serves to build confidence and agility. Use five to six bags. Care must be taken that this drill doesn't turn into a conditioning drill unless that is the express purpose of the drill.

Procedure: Linemen step two steps in each hole starting with the leg closest to the bag. Linemen work sideways over the bags.

Coaching Points for Players:
- Pump the arms.
- Keep the shoulders over the knees.
- Don't look down. (See bags with bottom of the eyes.)
- Burst at the end.
- Don't throw feet out to the side.

Weave

Purpose: Develops balance and lateral movement.

Procedure: Linemen align on the back tip of the first bag and work up, over, and back, as they come to the next bag.

Coaching Points for Players:
- Have good arm action.
- Keep the shoulders over the knees.
- Don't cross the feet.
- Keep eyes up.
- Square off turns. (Don't round off.)
- Burst at the back of each bag as you work forward again.

Z Drill

Purpose: Teaches defensive linemen how to redirect as they work forward. Foot agility, balance, and coordination are emphasized.

Procedure: Linemen work the length of the bags by moving forward with a zigzag shuffle at each bag.

Coaching Points for Players:
- Don't cross the feet. (Shuffle keeping feet close to the ground.)
- Keep the shoulders square.
- Keep eyes up.
- Work the arms.

360-Degree Turn

Purpose: Evaluates a lineman's balance and agility. Also develops the lineman's ability to locate the ball during a play or on a pass rush move.

Procedure: Have a line of players 15 yards from the coach. On command, the player will sprint toward the coach. On the second command, the lineman will execute a 360-degree turn and sprint past the coach.

Coaching Points for Players:
- The spin must be tight.
- Sink the hips.
- Throw the elbow *opposite* the turn into the turn. (Keep the elbow close to the body.)
- Keep the head up and get eyes around quickly.

Two-Point Wave

Purpose: Acts as a measuring stick for agility, reaction, and mobility skills or develops and/or refines those skills.

Procedure: Lineman faces a coach who has a ball in his hands. The coach uses the ball to direct the lineman sideways, forward, or backwards.

Coaching Points for Players:
- Avoid crossover with the feet.
- Stay low.
- Keep feet close to the ground.
- Drive hips down.

Stance Drills

Note: In addition to using the two stance drills in this section, you can observe and refine stance in any drill.

Stance

Purpose: Ensures defensive linemen are in a proper base stance or variable stances, such as psycho, taco, blast, ricochet, tab, etc.

Procedure: Have players align against a landmark. Call out various alignments or movements. Check stances for each. Check for flat back, tail slightly higher than shoulders, and proper weight distribution.

Transition

Purpose: Teaches linemen how to move to or transition from one stance to another (e.g., move from a right-handed to a left-handed stance).

Procedure: Have players align on landmarks in a stance. On a "move" call the defensive lineman will move to an opposite stance (e.g., right stance to a left stance).

Takeoff Drills

Some of these drills are performed against air, while others require a service person. These drills are initiated on ball movement.

One-Step Get-Off

Purpose: Teaches defensive linemen to take a proper first step. Focus on a six-inch first step with the knee over the toes, chest over the knee, and Z in the knees (leverage). Throw hands forward with thumbs up.

Procedure: Linemen line up against markers, and on ball movement take one step and freeze to allow coach to critique the step.

Perfect Fit

Purpose: Teaches how to get proper leverage on a blocker with head in the clavicle, hands on the breastplate and sleeve with thumbs up and elbows in.

Procedure: One-on-one setup with offensive man on knees. On ball movement the defensive lineman will attack the offensive blocker. The defender will freeze to allow the coach to check fit.

Get-Off (Chutes)

Purpose: Teaches linemen correct get-off with a low pad level.

Procedure: Place an agile bag or board in a chute with linemen crowding the bag. On ball movement each lineman explodes out of his stance with a low pad level. The linemen keep the pad between their legs.

Get-Off vs. Bodies

Purpose: Teaches defenders how to properly execute get-off techniques.

Procedure: Align offensive linemen five yards away from a group of defenders. The offensive linemen align in a two-point stance and backpedal when the ball is snapped. The defensive linemen fire out on ball movement and sprint to the retreating offensive linemen. Defenders tap the service man when they catch them.

Coaching Points for Players:
- See the ball in the peripheral vision.
- Move the down hand when the ball moves.
- Stay low.
- Pump the arms.
- Move on ball movement.

Takeoff/Redirect

Purpose: Marries the base takeoff drill with a wave or redirection drill.

Procedure: Linemen execute a takeoff drill, whether it is a simple takeoff drill or alignment/takeoff drill, followed with a redirection move.

Line Step

Purpose: Teaches outside shades how to step straight ahead on power step. One of the main reasons outside shades are reached is they step toward the middle of the offensive man they are aligned on instead of stepping straight ahead.

Procedure: Pair up two defenders with one man designated as the offensive or service man. Align a defensive man with his shaded foot on a yard line. Position the service man according to the shade you want the defensive man to have. For example, if you want a foot-to-foot alignment place the service man's foot on the line also. Should a foot-to-crotch alignment be desired adjust the service man's position so his crotch is on the yard line. On movement the defensive man simply steps into the service man. His power step should hit the yard line. If his step is to the service man's side of the line the defender is stepping *into* the offensive lineman and as a result will be reached more easily.

One-on-One Get-Off

Purpose: Teaches defensive linemen to get off on movement and close the gap.

Procedure: Place an offensive lineman on a line facing a defender. Behind the line, place a cone five yards deep. On movement, have the offensive man backpedal. The defender must close the gap and touch the offensive man before the service man gets to the cone.

Slant and Redirect

Purpose: Educates defensive linemen on slanting, reading the blocking scheme and redirecting.

Procedure: A defender faces three offensive linemen. The defender aligns on the middle man. On movement, have the defender slant right or left. The offensive linemen are instructed to zone right or left. Defensive reaction depends upon which way he is slanting and which way the offense is zoning.
- Zoning to: The defender must not be reached or redirected. He must work flat down the line.
- Zoning away: Avoid being reached by the adjacent lineman. Redirect playside.

Coaching Points for Players:
- Narrow the stance slightly.
- Mentally place weight on the foot opposite the initial step.
- Penetrate first.
- Aiming point is near hip of adjacent lineman.

Two Bag Goal Line Charge

Purpose: Teaches linemen how to tough charge in a short yardage or goal line situation.

Procedure: This drill is similar to the tough charge drill except two bags are butted together with the lineman's face in the crack. On ball movement the defender explodes through the two pads splitting them.

Tough Charge

Purpose: Teaches linemen how to tough charge in a short yardage or goal line situation.

Procedure: Place a lineman in a tough stance on a yard line. On the other side of the yard line place an agile bag. The lineman lines up with his face on the bag. On ball movement the defender will execute a low charge with his face on the bag and good hip roll. He will drive the bag upfield and work to his feet.

Contact Drills

Contact drills include many hands-only drills. Two-, four-, and six-point stances are used. Some drills include the use of a live opponent, sleds, or shiver balls. A hand circuit with nine segments is included. A short steer series is also included.

Quick Draw

Purpose: Teaches defensive linemen how to quickly shoot their hands to a target.

Procedure: Defenders pair up. They shade each other to one side with the shaded foot splitting the crotch of the partner. Each defender should have good knee bend with their hands to the side (holster). On ball movement or command each player tries to beat his competitor to the punch (draw his gun). Freeze defenders and check for correct hand placement with thumps up.

Cut

Purpose: Teaches defenders how to protect their legs versus cut type blocks. This drill is beneficial to any defensive position.

Procedure: Line up a series of agile bags, usually three to four bags, three yards apart, and have defenders work down the line hand shivering the bags which simulates offensive players throwing a low block. To instill an attack-the-line-of-scrimmage mentality, place the bags at an angle that forces the defender to gain ground as he progresses. Each defender starts from a bent knee position. As the defender shuffles down the line he hand shivers each bag. Defenders should avoid crossing their feet over. Teach defenders to keep their head up and see the bags with the bottom of the eyes. Defenders should keep flowside leg back as they work the line. Finish the drill with a form tackle, scoop and score, or fall on fumble. From here you can graduate to placing live bodies on all fours where the bags were and have them lunge and block, or grab the defender as he works down the line.

Strike/Dip/Thrust

Purpose: Accentuates power angles in the knees and an upward thrust into a blocker.

Procedure: Pair up defenders with a service man holding a bag. On ball movement the defender strikes the bag with a shoulder lift or hand shiver. On command the defender exaggerates knee bend. Hold him there two or three seconds, and on the second command the defender thrusts *upward* through the pad. If the defender uses a shoulder lift, he should fully extend his hands during the thrust part of the drill.

Four-Point Bench

Purpose: Teaches defensive linemen correct hand placement on an offensive man.

Procedure: Pair up defenders. Designate one player as an offensive lineman (service man) and one as the defender. The drill begins with both players on their knees. Shade the defender and have the service man simply fall forward. The defender has to hand shiver, with correct hand placement, and roll his hips. Check head and hand placement. The drill then progresses to the service man falling right or left which simulates a down or reach block. Again check hand placement and the defender's head in crack (HIC). The drill can evolve to the service man coming out from a three-point stance at a controlled speed with the defender still on his knees. This shows the defender the importance of a good hip roll and a short quick and full extension of the hands with elbows locked out.

Quick Hands

Purpose: Develops the hand quickness defensive linemen need to contact blockers.

Procedure: Have defenders on all fours in front of a sled. On ball movement the defender must get his hands as quickly as possible from the ground to the pad.

Six-Point Rapid Fire Hands

Purpose: Teaches defensive linemen that the strength of the hand shiver comes from the quickness of the blow.

Procedure: Linemen position themselves on their hand and knees in front of a sled pad. On ball movement the defenders hand shiver the pad and then reposition their hands quickly on the ground. Each cycle gets three to four rapid fire repetitions. This drill can progress to a six-point hand shiver with a hip roll. Additionally, defenders can align in a three-point stance with hand shiver and a good hip roll.

Piano

Purpose: Teaches defensive linemen how to hand shiver as they work down the line of scrimmage.

Procedure: A line of defenders align at the end of a five- or seven-man sled. Each defender shuffles down the line of pads. At each pad defenders will use a hand shiver.

Coaching Points for Players:
- Don't cross over when shuffling down the line.
- The strength of the blow comes from how quickly the hands extend.
- Don't allow any windups.
- Determine which foot to have back when working down the line.

Shiver Ball

Purpose: Teaches defenders how to play low or cut blocks in a safe manner.

Procedure: Each defender faces a shiver ball in a three-point stance. The coach shoves the ball toward the defender. The defender must hand shiver the ball to keep it off their lower body. Progress to where defenders shade the shiver ball. Roll the ball to the shaded side to simulate a reach block or away from the shade to mimic a down block.

Coaching Points for Players:
- Hit the ball with the heel of the hand.
- Play the block from the ground up.

- Don't wind up.
- Work both right and left stances.
- Finish the drill with a quick burst right or left.

Six-Point Contact

Purpose: Teaches defensive linemen how to attack on movement with correct head and hand placement. Also, this drill develops explosive hip snap.

Procedure: Defensive linemen face a sled or bag in a six-point stance (hands and knees). On movement, the defender will lead with his eyes and hands as his hips uncoil. The defender will end up on his belly if he executes correct hip extension and roll. Progress to a three-point stance contact drill with a lunge.

Coaching Points for Players:
- Curl the toes.
- There is no drive. (Just a lunge is required.)
- Hit on the rise.
- Face and hands should hit simultaneously.

Three-Point Contact and Drive

Purpose: Teaches a progression from the six-point contact drill.

Procedure: Instead of explosion only as in the six-point drill defenders will fire out from a three-point stance with the same eye and hand placement and will drive the sled or bag.

Pre-Lock Up Reach Reaction

Purpose: Teaches linemen how to turn a reach block into the sideline. Instead of coming out of a stance the defender will pre-lock up by starting out with correct hand placement. Both offensive and defensive men are in two point stances. A key to defeating a reach block is to run the offensive lineman's shoulders to where they face the sideline. This is done via a "long arm/short arm" technique by the defensive lineman.

Procedure: Defenders pair up with blockers in a two-point stance with hand placement already initiated. For drill purposes, the defender places his hands at the top of the blocker's numbers. The defender aligns in a pre-determined shade on the blocker. From this position the blocker will try to reach the defender. The defender will focus on throwing his hips outside and extending his playside arm (push) and pull the blocker with his inside arm. This action causes the blocker to expend his energy toward the sideline and away from the defender. The drill can end with an escape maneuver (rip or swim).

One-on-One Base Lockout

Purpose: Teaches the linemen to lockout a base block while keeping a good base.

Procedure: Blocker offsets the board while the defender aligns on the board. The blocker will execute a base block. The defender will squeeze the block while keeping a good base. The blocker should mix in a down block to keep the defender honest. Use steer technique. The defender should turn the blocker's shoulders to the point of attack. Long arm/inside arm.

Quick Hands

Purpose: Teaches players to develop quick hands without winding up and keeping hands tight on contact. Use a short, quick punch. Emphasize quick hands with no wind up. Hands should have tight placement with hands quick and inside.

Procedure: Two players face each other in a six-point stance. On ball movement they seek to out-quick each other with a hand shiver. The players can progress to a two-point stance.

Hand Circuit—#1: Lockout

Purpose: Develops a lineman's ability to use his hands.

Procedure: On his knees versus a dummy, the lineman places his hands at the appropriate place then locks out the elbows. This set-up gives the player the feeling of using his back muscles and not only his arms. He should use the hard part of his hand. His head and shoulder level should be low and constant. He should focus his eyes straight on the target.

Hand Circuit—#2: Lockout and Hips

Purpose: Develops the feel of lockout with hip roll.

Procedure: Players lock out, then roll hips.

Hand Circuit—#3: Full Engage

Purpose: Develops total hand shiver technique.

Procedure: Players perform a six-point explosion on movement. Strength of blow comes from:
- Quickness of hands (No wind up or double clutch.)
- Locking of elbows
- Rolling of hips
- Not a slap, but a blow

Many of the hand circuit ideas were developed by the late Fritz Shurmur, a longtime NFL defensive coordinator.

Hand Circuit—#4: Three-Point Lockout and Hip Extension

Purpose: Develops lockout and hands from a three-point stance.

Procedure: The player gets in a three-point stance and places his hands on a sled. On movement, he locks out and rolls the hips. He should not move his feet.

Hand Circuit—#5: Full Engage From Stance, No Step

Purpose: Teaches contact, fit, explosion, and hip roll from a three-point stance.

Procedure: The player starts in a three-point stance and on movement attacks the pad with good technique. No step is used. Elevation of shoulder and eyes should be constant.

Hand Circuit—#6: Total Engagement With Step

Purpose: Develops all the ingredients of blow delivery.

Procedure: The player locks out, rolls his hips, and finishes with a short step with shaded foot. The sequence is strike and step. It cannot be done simultaneously.

Hand Circuit—#7: Hands vs. Blocker

Purpose: Transfers what was learned versus pads to a live blocker.

Procedure: Pair up a blocker with a defensive man in a three-point stance. The blocker is in a two-point stance with his hands on his knees. The defensive man attacks with various amounts of resistance, starting with little or no resistance. He should drive or walk the offensive player back, keeping his shoulder and face mask level lower than the offensive man.

Hand Circuit—#8: Hands vs. Blocker

Purpose: Develops hands technique versus blocker coming out of stance.

Procedure: Linemen pair up with offensive men. The offensive players come out of their stance with various speeds.

Hand Circuit—#9: Hands With Shed

Purpose: Develops hand skills with disengage. Can end up with a tackle drill.

Procedure: The lineman pairs up with a blocker. A runner is also used in this drill. The defender starts in a three-point stance. He should force the blocker back until the ballcarrier makes his move. Then, he disengages and finishes with a tackle. He should continue to press the blocker back until the back makes a move.

Steer Series—#1: Short Steer

Purpose: Teaches defenders how to steer away from his gap responsibility when he is in a perfect fit with leverage. Drill is used primarily for playside reaction (i.e., base turnout or base).

Procedure: Two players pre-lock up in a perfect fit with leverage. On the command "fit-steer," the defender will steer away from gap responsibility.

Steer Series—#2: Long Steer

Purpose: Teaches the defender how to steer away from his gap responsibility. Similar to short steer except will add an escape.

Procedure: Use the same set-up described for the short steer drill, but the defender will crossface the blocker with a drop step and perform a rip, swim, or crossface wipe and pursuit.

Separation/Escape Drills

Since separating and escaping from a blocker are so intertwined, they are combined in this section.

Separation

Purpose: Teaches defensive linemen how to lockout arms and roll the hips to gain separation.

Procedure: Pair up defenders on all fours. Designate who is on defense and shade the service man. The service man leans into the defender giving him pressure. Have the defense man place his hands on the pec and cuff with his elbows bent. On command, have the defender bench the offensive man and roll his hips. The defensive man should end up with his elbows in a locked position and separation from the blocker.

Escape

Purpose: Teaches a defensive player how to engage, control and escape an offensive blocker.

Procedure: The defender aligns on the one man sled. On ball movement the defender will attack and lockout the sled. When the defender controls the sled, he will step through the gap while ripping with the inside arm.

One-Man Shed Disengage

Purpose: Instills in defenders the confidence and ability to engage and control a block and then escape.

Procedure: A line of defenders face a one man or popsicle sled. On movement the defender attacks the sled, locks out and then escapes in a predetermined direction. The drill can simulate an escape with the ball near, a few gaps away, or far outside. Defenders then leave the sled at the prescribed angle using a rip, crossface wipe, or snatch. Place a jersey on the sled so defenders have cloth to grasp and manipulate.

Escape

Purpose: Teaches the mechanics of escaping blockers.

Procedure: Pair up two defenders against bags or a two man sled. On movement the defenders will execute contact on the sled or bag and will escape to their outside. It is beneficial to have the defender on the left to be on a right handed stance and the defender on the right to be in a left handed stance. This allows defenders to get work on both right and left stances. Drill rip, crossface wipe, and snatch escape techniques.

Lock Up/Escape/Form Tackle

Purpose: Teaches linemen to fight pressure, lockout, separate and make a form tackle.

Procedure: Blocker and lineman pre-lock up with lineman's hands inside with the blocker's hands outside in a good, flexed football position. The blocker drives the defender until the defender locks out and separates to make the play.

Pursuit Drills

Defensive success usually hinges on the desire and discipline of the defense as they stalk the ball and make the tackle. These drills foster a good mental attitude about running to the ball and teach proper angles linemen should use. Run and pass pursuit drills are included.

Lateral Pursuit

Purpose: Teaches linemen to play the runner inside-out.

Procedure: A defender lines up with inside leverage on a ballcarrier. On command, the ballcarrier runs to a cone or sideline while the lineman performs a defensive run with his shoulders and hips square to the ballcarrier. When the ballcarrier turns to the line of scrimmage, the defender presses and tackles the runner.

Wide Play Run Angles

Purpose: Teaches linemen correct angles as they pursue the ball.

Procedure: Align linemen in various fronts using cones as offensive linemen. On ball movement, have a "rabbit" with a ball run wide. Defensive linemen step with the correct foot and use good inside out angles to the ball seeking to two-hand touch the ballcarrier below the waist. Linemen should not follow the same color. This drill can be used against air, cones, or an offensive line that gives the defense half-speed blocks.

Redirect and Burst

Purpose: Teaches get-off and redirecting for run or pass plays without fish hook angles.

Procedure: Linemen go in pairs. At the get-off, the coach will point to particular cones. Defensive linemen must redirect with sharp angles and sprint to those cones.

Pass Rush vs. Air/Rush—Retrace/Pursue

Purpose: Teaches exit angles and pursuit lanes on downfield pass, screens, plus squeeze and retrace technique on draws.

Procedure: Linemen stay in rush lanes and adjust to a screen, downfield passes, and draws.

Quick Pass Pursuit

Purpose: Teaches defenders how to convert from a pass rush mode to a good pursuit angle on the receiver.

Procedure: Align defenders on the line of scrimmage with service personnel aligned across from them holding bags or shields. On the snap, have these service men try to hit the defenders knee high with the bags. This simulates an offensive lineman cutting the defender in an attempt to get his hands down. A quarterback will throw the ball to one of a series of receivers which have been strategically placed in the flat areas. Defenders must play the block from the ground up and pursue at the correct angle.

Screen Pass Pursuit

Purpose: Teaches linemen how to break off their pass rush and collapse on the receiver.

Procedure: Defenders should understand that the angles they will take are similar to angles they would take on a wide running play. As with a running play, defenders should not follow the same colored jersey.

Tackling/Turnover Drills

This section includes tackling and turnover drills since they are so closely related. Defensive linemen seldom will make the picture-perfect tackle that linebackers or defensive backs make because they are in a very congested area of the field. However, any tackle by a defensive lineman is crucial since they usually happen at or close to the inception of a play.

Tackling should be taught slowly until players master the technique and overcome a natural fear of contact. The old adage that 90 percent of tackling is desire may be true but you still have to teach the 10 percent technique and help foster the desire. Two important elements in tackling include: bending at the knees and keeping the head up. "See what you hit" is good advice.

Tackling Progression

Purpose: Teaches defenders how to properly tackle using a progression approach. The progression teaches tackling in reverse order.

Procedure:
- *Step 1:* Put the tackler in a good "fit" position, grabbing cloth. Have the ballcarrier hold a ball. This fit should result in the tackler either having his face or shoulder pad on the ball.
- *Step 2:* The tackler is still in the "fit" position except his arms are hanging loosely to his sides. On command, have the tackler shoot his hands to wrap up grabbing cloth.
- *Step 3:* Have the tackler fit in as illustrated in Step 2. On command, have the defender shoot his hands to wrap up *and* incorporate a hip roll.
- *Step 4:* Have the tackler in a football position one step away from the ballcarrier. On command, he executes a full-speed tackle complete with placing his eyes or shoulder on the ball, shooting the hands, hip roll, and foot acceleration. Obviously, for safety reasons, he should not take the ballcarrier to the ground.

Shed and Tackle

Purpose: Simulates game conditions for the lineman, i.e., just after the defender disengages from a blocker.

Procedure: A defender faces off with a blocker in a five yard area marked with cones. Behind the blocker is a ballcarrier. The blocker will fire out at the defender at half speed. (This is a tackling drill and not a shed drill.) The defender will take on the blocker, shed him and make a form tackle on the ballcarrier. The defender can work in a head-up position or a shade. If in a head-up position, the ballcarrier has a two-way go. In a shade, the runner must run to the defender's shade.

Goal Line Tackle

Purpose: Teaches the defender how to tackle near the goal line.

Procedure: The defender starts out with his heels on the goal line facing a ballcarrier. Between the defender and the ballcarrier is a bag placed parallel to the goal line. On command, the defender buzzes his feet. The ballcarrier can run right or left. The defender must wrap up high and drive his feet.

Tackle/Turnover Circuit

Purpose: Teaches defenders how to tackle in different situations. It also teaches how to force turnovers. Also included is indoctrination on how to react to differing game situations. This drill can be done throughout the season.

Procedure: This drill can be done in both five- and ten-minute segments. You can usually have four different stations from day to day. Following are the advantages to this setup:
- You get a phenomenal amount of repetitions in a short period.
- Each coach sees every defensive player sometime during the circuit. (This helps with evaluation.)
- Linemen get to tackle quality ballcarriers as opposed to tackling only in their group.
- It is a good way to teach the nuances of the game.

Following are some of the drills to use in tackling/turnover circuits:
- Tackling
  - ✓ Form
  - ✓ Angle
  - ✓ Sideline
  - ✓ Roll
  - ✓ Goal line
  - ✓ Open field
  - ✓ Head up
  - ✓ Blind side on quarterback
  - ✓ Quarterback scramble
  - ✓ Desperation
  - ✓ Shed tackle
  - ✓ Square tackle
  - ✓ Eye opener
  - ✓ Peel
- Turnovers
  - ✓ Strip (tomahawk ballside; punch offside)
  - ✓ CPR (club-punch-rip)
  - ✓ Fumble fall on technique
  - ✓ Fumble scoop and score technique
  - ✓ Fumble if behind in score
  - ✓ Fumble if ahead in score
  - ✓ Interception
  - ✓ Interception if behind in score
  - ✓ Interception if ahead in score
  - ✓ Hockey drill
  - ✓ Blind man's bluff

Pass Rush Drills

Included are drills which are run from a pre-lock up position, against air, against an opponent, or with cones. Draw and screen drills are incorporated in order to teach linemen how to react if they read a screen or draw. Some drills are in series.

Quarterback Run-By

Purpose: Teaches defensive linemen (ends) how to rush the quarterback but not run by him because of centrifugal force.

Procedure: Set up two cones five yards apart. Have the defender lean into the first cone and run *around* the second cone. Timing this drill can foster competition.

Knife and Gun

Purpose: Teaches hand speed for pass rushing.

Procedure: Pair up a pass protector with a pass rusher. The offensive man should use a mix of knife and gun moves.

- *Gun*: Offensive man reaches from the hip like he is pulling a gun. The defender either slaps his hands down or inside.
- *Knife*: Offensive man extends from the shoulders with the defensive man lower. The defensive man will slap or work the offensive man's hands high.

Pass Rush Progression

Purpose: Teaches rushers basic pass rush moves using the upper body only.

Procedure: A rusher and protector face off while on both knees. On the offensive man's movement the rusher will attack and seek to execute a rip or swim move. The offensive man will seek to get hands inside the rusher. The next step would be to do the same drill with participants in a two-point stance. The rusher will add footwork in this segment.

Blind Bull Rush

Purpose: Teaches pass rushers how to *feel* the pass protector leaning into the rusher. When a pass protector leans or scotches he is susceptible to a pass rush move. Effective pass rushers must be able to *feel* this lean.

Procedure: Pair up a pass rusher and pass protector in a pre-lock up mode. Have the rusher bull rush the blocker. At some point have the blocker lean or scotch into the rusher. The rusher should have a blindfold or execute the rush with his eyes closed so he can only detect this lean or shift by feel.

Two-on-One Pass Rush

Purpose: Reveals which defenders have an all-out attitude in rushing the quarterback; improves conditioning.

Procedure: The drill begins with a pass rusher facing one pass protector. The second pass protector doesn't become involved until if and when the rusher defeats the first blocker. The second blocker doesn't become involved until the rusher *totally* disengages with the first blocker. When the first blocker is defeated, he is disqualified from any further participation in the drill.

Draw/Screen vs. Air

Purpose: Teaches defensive linemen how to react when they read draw or screen.

Procedure: Align defensive linemen in positions with a quarterback holding a ball. Have the quarterback drop level three. If simulating a draw the quarterback will lower the ball from shoulder level to waist high. Defenders yell *"Draw! Draw!,"* plant their outside foot and open up to the inside. Defenders retrace their steps looking back inside. If the quarterback gets an abnormal drop defenders should yell *"Screen! Screen!."* Defenders look outside first, then to the middle. Service receivers can be placed in the flat and middle areas if the coach wants to add an actual throw.

Bull Rush

Purpose: Allows the pass rusher to get a feel of a power or bull rush with the defender never scotching or transferring his weight forward; educates the rusher how to identify the point when a pass rusher scotches or transfers his weight into the rusher.

Procedure: A pass rusher faces an offensive blocker in a pre-lock up position. On command, the rusher will start powering the blocker backward. The offensive man gives ground grudgingly but never tries to stop the defenders forward movement. A pass rusher in this position always continues on his pass rush. After each defender gets a feel of powering the blocker backward he is ready to move to the second part of the drill. The second time through the pass protector will scotch or stonewall the pass rusher. This gives the pass rusher the experience of feeling a weight transfer by the pass protector. At this point, the pass protector is ripe for a push/pull move.

Pass Rush vs. Air

Purpose: Exposes pass rushers to the technique needed to execute a rip or swim pass rush move against air. Going against air initially helps build confidence.

Procedure: Line up linemen—as many as you can watch—down a yard line. Have them work—all at the same time—forward executing the prescribed swim or rip move at their own pace.

Coaching Points for Players:
- Make sure the same arm and leg work together.
- When executing the rip, sink the hips, roll the trunk to the sky and visualize placing the top of the rip shoulder under the imaginary blocker's armpit.
- The swim should be more of a stab over an imaginary shoulder as opposed to an elongated 12 o'clock move.

Pass Rush Down the Line

Purpose: Educates pass rushers how to execute a pass rush move at a leisurely pace against bodies. This drill is a metamorphosis of the pass rush vs. air drill.

Procedure: A pass rusher works down a line of four to five bodies who offer token resistance. The rusher, at a good learning pace, executes the prescribed pass rush move. The men move up one man so a rotation is established.

Takeoff

Purpose: Instructs pass rushers the value of good takeoff and lean on a pass rush assignment.

Procedure: Place a cone four yards to the right and left of a football. This simulates the line of scrimmage. Place two cones four yards deep and one yard inside the original cones. Mark the quarterback's launch point with a cone seven yards deep directly over the football. Place defenders in line on the cones to the right and left on the line of scrimmage. On ball movement, have one side rush. Alternate sides with defenders rotating to get work on both sides. Defenders should use good takeoff technique and lean at the second cone that is placed four yards deep. At the second cone, defenders should work to get their toes pointed to the launch point. This drill can be timed or can be used in a competitive manner by having two pass rushers going at the same time.

Pre-Lock Up Rip

Purpose: Trains pass rushers how to execute a rip pass rush move from a pre-lock up position.

Procedure: Pre-lock up a pass protector and a pass rusher. On command have the pass protector retreat. The pass rusher leans into the offensive man while the blocker pushes him. The pass rusher will grab cloth behind the blockers outside shoulder and pushes. The rusher will throw the rip seeking to get the top of his shoulder under the blocker's armpit. The rusher should roll his trunk to the sky as he tries to touch his ear with the rip arm's thumb.

Hoops

Purpose: Drills pass rushers how to keep their cleats in the ground while running with a low center of gravity as they maintain balance and body lean.

Procedure: The hoop or circle drawn on the ground should be ten to twelve feet in circumference. Have the pass rusher align in a three-point stance and on ball movement run the hoops keeping a good body lean. As the defender finishes one circuit of the hoops have him burst past a cone placed near the starting point. Occasionally place a player on, or coach inside, the hoop and have him give the rusher a shove. This shove teaches the value of a good lean with a low inside shoulder. Two hoops can be placed side by side. Have the rusher run a figure-eight course.

Pre-Lock Up High Hand Counter

Purpose: Schools a pass rusher how to cope when a pass blocker grabs the rusher high on a swim move.

Procedure: Pre-lock up a blocker and rusher. As the rusher executes a swim move have the blocker grab him high on the pads. The rusher at this point will convert to a rip by taking the off (outside) hand and push up on the blocker's outside elbow while transitioning to a rip. The rusher will lean and run the edge.

Pass Rush vs. Air/Rush Lanes

Purpose: Teaches proper rush lanes spill and cage responsibilities, aim points on the quarterback and rushing against a moving pocket.

Procedure: Linemen stay in assigned rush lanes. A and B gap rushers attack the quarterback's near shoulder while C and D gap rushers attack the quarterback's back shoulder.

Pre-Lock Up Low Hand Counter

Purpose: Teaches the pass rusher a counter move off a rip move versus a blocker using a low grab.

Procedure: Pre-lock up a pass blocker and a pass rusher. Have the rusher use a rip pass rush move and instruct the pass blocker to clamp down and sit on the rip with a low grab. The rusher at this point will pull at the rip and convert to a swim move.

Rush vs. Stand-Up Dummies

Purpose: Teaches linemen the mechanics of a pass rush move.

Procedure: Four stand-up dummies are used. These dummies are placed eight yards apart. Each rusher will approach a dummy and make the required pass rush move. Rushers will burst after each move and come to balance as they approach the next dummy. Go in groups of four and then rotate.

Get-Off vs. Bodies

Purpose: Teaches defensive linemen how to get off quickly versus a body on a pass rush.

Procedure: Defensive lineman lines up against an offensive lineman who is in a two- or three-point stance. On ball movement the rusher will rush and turn the corner versus the offensive lineman who doesn't move. Vary the launch point. Use three-, five-, and seven- step launch points.

Lockup Series—#1: Pre-Lock Up Rip

Purpose: Teaches linemen how to execute a rip pass rush move.

Procedure: Rusher pairs up with a blocker. From there he executes a rip.

Lockup Series—#2: (Pass Rush) Pre-Lock Up Rip/Counter-Pick

Purpose: Teaches rushers how to counter move off the rip pass rush.

Procedure: Blocker places his outside arm high on the rusher. The rusher will execute the "pick" by lifting that arm up with his outside arm as he steps through. The hips are under the shoulders. The blocker is lifted by hips of the rusher. Point toes to the quarterback.

Lockup Series—#3: Pre-Lock Up Rip/Counter-Spin

Purpose: Teaches linemen how to counter move off a rip pass rush when the blocker overextends outside.

Procedure: Offensive lineman and defensive lineman pre-lock up with the blocker overextended. The rusher, when he feels pressure from the blocker's opposite hand, will pivot off his inside leg with a discus throw with the outside arm. The spin must be tight.

Speed Rush Series—#1: Speed Rush

Purpose: Teaches pass rushers the mechanics of the speed rush.

Procedure: From a pre-lock up position the rusher locks up with a pass protector. From a lockup, he leans and runs.

Speed Rush Series—#2: Speed Rush Counter

Purpose: Teaches pass rushers the mechanics of the counter off the speed rush.

Procedure: From a pre-lock up have the rusher lean and run. Have the blocker slip his head upfield as far as the rusher's outside shoulder. At this point, the rusher should execute a swim or rip counter move to the inside. The rusher should club or pull with his inside hand on the blockers inside half.

Power Rush Series—#1: Power Rush

Purpose: Pre-lock up with rusher getting the feel of a power rush.

Procedure: Players pair up, with a rusher power rushing against a blocker who offers minimal resistance.

Power Rush Series—#2: Power Rush

Purpose: Teaches rusher how to recognize when the blocker scotches on a power rush. The rusher will execute a "pull" move.

Procedure: Pre-lock up like #1 in series. At some point the blocker will scotch, at which point the rusher will execute the "pull" move with a rip or swim move.

Power Rush Series—#3: Hip Flip/Power Rush

Purpose: Teaches rushers how to execute a hip flip pass rush move.

Procedure: The rusher pairs up with a blocker. The rusher aligns one yard away from the blocker. The rusher will then attack with a quick explosive three-point contact causing the blocker to lean forward to brace. At this moment, the rusher will pull the blocker's shoulders down and inside and at the same time flip his hips to the outside. The hip-flip will be followed by a rip or swim depending upon the blocker's elevation.

Pass Cut

Purpose: Teaches defensive linemen to play off a cut block, recover, and react to knock down a pass by jumping and extending arms in front of the quarterback.

Procedure: Defensive linemen shuffle from bag to bag reaching and shivering the bags. The coach at some point will give pass indicators. Defenders then explode upward to affect the pass.

Draw

Purpose: Teaches rushers how to retrace steps versus a draw play.

Procedure: Two ends execute an upfield pass rush. The quarterback can either execute a pass drop or simulate a draw.

Screen

Purpose: Teaches rushers how to react to screen plays.

Procedure: Four rushers execute a pass rush and react to screens. When defenders recognize screen they plant the foot away from the screen and pursue in a good pursuit angle. Never follow the same color. The end to the screen should be cut using a shield.

Read Drills

One-on-one, two-on-one, and three-on-one reads are included. Inside and outside shades are drilled.

One-on-One Run/Pass Read

Purpose: Teaches linemen to transfer from anticipating a run reaction into a pass rush move.

Procedure: Offensive lineman is in a three-point stance. He will execute a run-type block (reach, down, base) or a pass set.

Two-on-One Run Reads

Purpose: Teaches linemen different combinations of two-on-one blocks (outside shades).

Procedure: Offensive men use base, scoop, double team, and pull collision blocks.

Three-on-One Two-Way Escape

Purpose: Teaches defensive linemen how to react when their alignment man pulls (pull collision blocks). The defensive linemen will read head placement of the blocker. If the head is upfield—crossface. If the head is downfield—backdoor.

Procedure: Coach gives alignment key direction. He will give signal for head placement by assigned blocker. Mix in base block to keep defender honest and in an attack mode.

One-on-One Read

Purpose: Educates defenders on how to react against the various one-on-one blocks they will see. This is also a good drill to *mentally* pre-snap read the stance the offensive lineman is in. This drill is good to work on both outside and inside shades. These drills can be done in shells, shorts, or pads.

Procedure: Pair up one offensive man facing a defender. Have the offensive man give clear and easily read visual cues as to the type of block he will be executing. For example the blocker can lean on a reach block or down block or be in a light stance as in a pass set. Versus outside shades the blocker should show the four basic blocks: base, down, reach, and pass. Versus inside shades the blocker should show: base, outside release, shoeshine, and pass.

Two-on-One Read

Purpose: Educates defenders on how to react against the various two-on-one blocks they will see.

Procedure: This drill is similar to the one-on-one read drill except the defender is faced by two blockers. The offensive blockers are controlled by a coach who stands behind the defender. The blockers should execute the basic two-on-one blocks:
- Double-team
- Power slip
- Power scrape
- Inside fold
- Outside fold

The offensive man should give easy-to-read tip-offs as to the type of blocks to be employed. Stance, splits, leans in stances, and on-the-ball and off-the-ball cues should be used to illustrate how easily pre-snap reads can be used by an observant defensive lineman.

Two-Point Mirror (Outside Shades/Inside Shades)

Purpose: Drills players on quick reactions to various blocks.

Procedure: Place defender on the blocker in a two-point power base stance. The defender will react to various blocks for two steps. For example:
- Outside shades: Base, base turnout, reach, down, pass set
- Inside shades: Base, shoeshine, outside release, pass set

This drill can be used in three phases:
- Phase 1: No contact, just initial two-step movement
- Phase 2: Contact only to a fit
- Phase 3: Full contact—live

Three-Point Mirror (Outside Shades/Inside Shades)

Purpose: Drills players on quick reactions to various blocks.

Procedure: Place defender and blocker in proper three-point stances and have the defender react to various blocks. This drill can be used in three phases:
- Phase 1: No contact, just initial two-step movement
- Phase 2: Contact only to a fit
- Phase 3: Full contact—live

Coaching Points for Players:
- Watch steps
- Elbows back and tight
- Hands in the holster
- Leverage
- Perfect fit
- Hand placement
- Punch
- Thumbs on lockout
- Steer
- Squeeze
- Escape

Shoeshine

Purpose: Teaches linemen playing in an inside shade how to play a shoeshine block.

Procedure: Place a defender opposite a shiver ball near a board. The board will force the defender to keep his feet and hips back. Attempt to push the ball inside the defender simulating a shoeshine block.

Chase

Purpose: Teaches linemen proper chase techniques.

Procedure: Place defender backside. Execute these various plays away from the defender: ball away (down/high wall), blocks, counter, reverse, bootleg, pass set.

Slant Drills

Slant and Redirect

Purpose: Teaches linemen to slant, find the ball, and redirect.

Procedure: Linemen pair up with offensive men. Defensive man executes a slant. As linemen complete the slant, they get a direction from the coach. The lineman must flatten out.

Slant

Purpose: Teaches linemen how to read and react on a slant move.

Procedure: Two defensive tackles align on live bodies or cones which simulate guards. On the snap of the ball they slant in a pre-determined direction. A ballcarrier will give them play direction. The tackles step with the foot in the direction they are slanting and find the ballcarrier. They react to his direction and either flatten (if the ball is to them) or redirect (if the ball is away from them). Linemen should concentrate on movement first taking the proper steps, dipping and ripping, to penetrate the gap moving to.

Two-on-One Slant Reads

Purpose: Teaches slanter to key the next blocker as he stunts into the gap.

Procedure: If blocker pulls away the lineman continues on his path. If the blocker fires out or zones toward him he will use his hands, helmet, and pads to redirect and get in a correct pursuit angle.

Glossary

A

A Gap: The space between the center and guard.

Aiming Point: A visual point of attack.

Alley: The running lane from outside the end man on the line of scrimmage to the sideline.

Angle of Pursuit: The position of a defender in relationship to the ballcarrier.

Attack-Read Stance: A basic defensive line stance.

B

B gap: The space between the offensive guard and tackle.

Backdoor: An escape maneuver when the defender is beaten, or the blocker overcommits to the playside; the defender escapes inside the block.

Ball Call: A call to alert the defense that the ball is on the ground, or a pass has been thrown.

Base Block: A block to screen a defender by staying between the defender and the ball; the number one block to defeat.

Base Step: A step after a power step that enables the defensive linemen to keep a good foundation; the lineman's second step.

Bears: A defensive front with the linemen in a strong 33 look.

Blast: A 7 technique stunt.

Bootleg: A play where the quarterback goes away from backfield flow with the ball.

C

C gap: The space between the offensive tackle and end.

Cage: A term that tells a defensive lineman that he has contain on the quarterback on pass plays.

Change: A line pass rush game; a pick to the open end and a pop to the closed side.

Chase: A backside defensive end technique on runs away. The end thinks bootleg-counter-reverse (BCR), closes to the original spot of the ball, then through the ball to a pursuit angle.

Claw: A technique where the defensive man seeks to keep his head in the crack (HIC).

Cobra: A stunt or pass rush game.

Cobra In: A pass rush game where the ends "mush rush" the quarterback.

Cobra Out: A pass rush game where the tackles "mush rush" the quarterback.

Cobra Stance: A pass rush sprinter's stance.

Cocked: A tackle's 1 technique 45-degree alignment on the center.

Compress: A technique used to squeeze the blocker into an adjacent gap. Also called steer.

Co-Op Block: A block on a 6 technique, where the tight end will reach the 6 technique and slip off to the next level, with the offensive tackle taking over the block.

Counter Club: A counter pass rush move off a speed rush.

Counter Pull: A counter pass rush move off a power pass rush move.

Counter Rip: A counter pass rush move off a swim.

Counter Spin: A rip counter pass rush move.

Counter Swim: A rip counter pass rush move.

Credit Card Alignment: The defensive linemen crowding the line of scrimmage.

Crossface Wipe: An escape move used when the ball is two, or more, gaps removed.

Cutback: A designed, or ad lib, run where the ballcarrier starts in one direction, and then changes direction, to run against the grain.

Cut Block: A type of block where the offensive lineman seeks to block the defensive lineman at knee level; used mostly on quick three-step passes, or screens.

Cutoff Block: A block where the offensive lineman releases inside versus an outside shade, and then turns back in an attempt to prevent pursuit. Also called a high-wall block.

Cut Reach Block: A block where the blocker drives his head below the defender's knee level in an attempt to reach him.

D

D Gap: The space outside the offensive end.

Declared Ball: The point when the ballcarrier commits to run in a particular direction.

Delayed Pick: A read pass rush game triggered by a pass set.

Delayed Pop: A read pass rush game triggered by a pass set.

Deuce: A zone blitz technique where the defender drops over the #2 receiver.

Double Team: A blocking scheme where two offensive linemen block one defensive lineman.

Down/Down: A call to signify two down blocks by adjoining offensive linemen.

Draw: A running play off a pass look.

Drive Block: A one-on-one straight-forward block which seeks to knock the defensive lineman off the line of scrimmage. Also called a base block.

Dropback Pass: A level three pass action.

E

Eagle: A 7 technique stunt.

Ed Block: An angle block by the offensive tackle, and the tight end pulling inside. A pull-collision type block.

End: The weakside defensive end, away from the closed side.

End It: A defensive end stunt.

Escape: A method of disengagement from a blocker.

Explosive Play: A run, or pass, over 20 yards.

F

Fit: A pursuit technique where the defender fits between the end of the line offensive blocker and the defensive force man.

5 Technique: The outside shade on the offensive tackle.

Fold Blocks: A combination block by two contiguous offensive linemen; one lineman angle blocks the defender while the other pulls inside or outside. Is a pull-collision block.

Forearm-Shoulder Lift: A block protection technique where the defensive lineman uses the top of the shoulder and top of the arm.

4x1 Rule: The end rule versus a reach block; the end will work to a spot one yard outside the reacher and four yards deep.

4 Technique: The inside shade on the offensive tackle.

G

Gap: The split between offensive linemen, labeled using letters.

Gap Call: A defensive call which tells linemen to align in the gap to the called shade, instead of aligning on the offensive lineman.

Gapside Hand: An uncovered hand.

Gap Stance: A stance used in a gap charge.

George Block: A fold block where the guard blocks out, and the tackle pulls inside; inside fold. Is a pull-collision block.

Get-Off: An explosive movement by a defensive lineman, on ball or opponent movemcnt.

Ghost 6: A head-up alignment on an imaginary tight end.

Gut: A technique where a drop lineman zones over the final #3 receiver; used in zone blitz package.

H

Hand Shiver: A block protection technique using the hard part of the hands (i.e., palms and heel of the hand).

Hanging Huddle: The pre-snap huddle protocol.

Hat in the Crack: A term used to describe a defensive lineman's attempt to keep his helmet in his assigned gap.

High Hat: A pass read given by an offensive lineman.

Hip Flip: A pass rush move.

Hot: A term used to notify defensive linemen that an outside stunt will be run. "Hot" informs outside shades that they are free to go under base or pass blocks.

Hump: A pass rush move.

I

Influence Block: An attempt by the blocking scheme that seeks to lure defensive linemen upfield away from the point of attack, or to trap them.

Inside Counter: A counter pass rush move off a speed rush.

J

Jam: A 5 technique to the strength call stunt.

Jump Through Block: An offensive lineman releasing inside a defensive lineman to block a level two defender.

K

Key: An object that is focused on prior to snap of the football. It may be a person, the ball, a small part of the person, or a part of the offensive lineman's equipment.

Kick-Out Block: An inside-out block usually executed on a defensive end.

L

Lateral Step: A flat, initial step parallel to the line of scrimmage by a defensive lineman used in executing a slant or stunt.

Lead Foot: A foot that is moved first usually the foot closest to desired direction. (For example, if lineman desires to go right, he should step with his right foot first.)

Left: A strength call to the defense's left.

Level Two: The depth of the defense where the linebackers are.

Leverage: 1. A body position that allows a defender to offset an offensive lineman's strength or proper angle on a particular gap. 2. A pursuit angle where the defender works inside-out to the ball.

Lin: A pass rush game with the left inside defender having contain to the right.

Load: A pin, or outside-in block by an offensive man on an end of the line defender.

Lockout: A technique where the defensive lineman controls a blocker by straightening his arms, keeping separation between him and the offensive lineman.

Long Stick: A technique where the ends slant two gaps; used in zone blitz package.

Loose: A lineman aligning in a wide shade; foot-to-foot alignment instead of foot-to-crotch.

LOS: The line of scrimmage; imaginary line through the football.

Low Hat: A run read given by an offensive lineman.

M

Max Protection: A pass protection scheme where the tight end and backs stay in to block, usually resulting in a one or two-man route.

Mush Rush: A defender rushing the quarterback in a restrained manner; the defender has collateral responsibilities of playing screen, draw, or quarterback scramble.

N

Near Back: The closest running back to a defender.

Neutral Zone: The imaginary plane that extends through the ball, and cannot be crossed by the defense before the ball is snapped.

Nose: The defensive tackle away from the strength call or away from the closed side.

O

Olay: A nose or 1 technique stunt.

One Gap: A defender who is responsible for only one gap; this gap is usually on the edge of a particular offensive player.

1 Technique: A shade on the center; if the 1 technique is to the call, it is referred to as a +1 alignment. If the 1 technique is away from the call, it is tagged as a -1 technique.

Out/Out Block: A blocking scheme where the tight end and offensive tackle both block the next man to their outside.

Over: A defensive front where the tackles are in a 31 alignment.

Over G: A defensive front where the tackles are in a 32 alignment.

Over Strong: A 2 technique to the call.

Over Weak: A 2 technique away from the call.

P

Pancake: A technique used to neutralize a double-team block; the defender drops to all fours—belly first—whenever he feels he is being driven to the second level.

Penetrator: A defender who is assigned to attack first in a two or three-man game.

Pick: A pass rush game incorporating lane exchanges, where the end goes first and the tackle goes second.

Pirate: A coordinated stunt between a 3 technique tackle, and the end.

Pop: A pass rush game incorporating lane exchanges, where the tackle goes first and the end goes second.

Power Hand: A gap responsibility-side hand.

Power Step: An initial six- to eight-inch step by the shaded foot.

Pressure: An area of most resistance given by a blocker; defenders—when in doubt—should always fight pressure.

Pull Lane: The area just behind the offensive line; many inside-out blocks originate in this area.

Pursuit: A fanatical effort to get to the ball, by taking the shortest and most direct path to the ball; essential to good defensive play.

Q

Quick: A 2 technique stunt.

Quick Chase: A pursuit technique for a 2 or 4 technique on plays away; the defender's thought process in playing this block is play from the ground up (Think fumbled snap to cutback).

R

Reach Block: A block where an offensive man seeks to gain outside leverage on an outside shaded defender.

Retrace: A technique where defensive linemen reverse pass rush steps when they read draw (i.e., they go back the way they went in).

Reverse: A play where the ball goes in a direction opposite of the initial flow.

Ricochet: A stunt where a 9 technique works inside to a 7 technique on the snap.

Right: A strength call to the right.

Rin: A pass rush game with the right inside defender having contain to the left.

Rip: A pass rush technique; also, a block-escape technique.

Rush Lane: A designated pass rush lane.

S

Scoop: A blocking scheme where a blocker seeks either inside or outside leverage with help from an adjacent offensive lineman.

Separation: An attempt to keep arm's length from a blocker.

7 Technique: An inside shade alignment on the tight end.

Sink Call: A call by defensive linemen to linebackers when they want to control an abnormal split by moving into the gap.

6 Technique: A head-up alignment on the tight end.

Snatch: A block escape move when the defender is far removed from the point of attack.

Speed Rush: A pass rush technique where the rusher seeks to out run a pass protector to the quarterback.

Spike: A 3 technique stunt.

Spill: A technique used when defenders take on an inside-out block and seek to have the ball bounce and not hit the seam.

Split: A nose's 3 technique to the call.

Spin: A last resort escape move.

Spin Rush: A pass rush move.

Sprint Out: A level two pass action with the quarterback attacking the corner with a pass/run option.

Spy: A technique where a defender or defenders "mush rush" the quarterback while playing screen/draw/quarterback scramble.

Square: A body position where defenders keep shoulders and butt parallel to the line of scrimmage.

Squeeze: A technique where defenders force a blocker into an adjacent gap while protecting his own gap.

Staggered Stance: A heel-to-toe alignment.

Steer Technique: A technique used to squeeze or steer a blocker away from a defender's gap responsibility.

Stem: An individualized movement by a defender or defenders to a new alignment or front.

Stick: A lineman slanting one gap.

Stick To Cage: A lineman slanting outside with cage responsibility; used in zone blitz scheme.

Strong: A 1 technique to the call.

Stunt Stance: A stance used on a stunt change.

Stud: A strongside defensive end.

Swim: A pass rush move.

T

Tab: A 4 technique stunt.

Tackle: The defensive tackle to the strength call, or closed side.

Taco: A 5 technique—away from the call—stunt.

3 Technique: An alignment on the outside shade of the guard.

Tug Block: A fold block, where the tackle blocks down and the guard pulls to the outside; an outside fold block.

Tough Stance: A short yardage or goal line stance.

Trail Hand: A release or shaded hand.

Trap Block: An inside-out block preceded by an influence or down block.

Turn Back Block: A blocking technique where the center check-back blocks for a guard who pulls across the ball.

Twist: A lane exchange game between the tackles.

2x1 Rule: A tackle's rule versus a reach block. The tackle will work to a spot one yard outside the reacher and two yards deep.

Two-Gap: A defender who is responsible for immediate gaps to the right and left; the defensive lineman aligns head up on the offensive lineman.

2 Technique: An inside alignment on the guard.

U

Under: A defensive front where the tackles are in a 13 alignment.

Under G: A defensive front where the tackles are in a 23 alignment.

W

Weak: A 1 technique away from the strength call.

Weak Bears: A defensive front with the linemen in a weak 33 look.

Wham Block: A trap block on a defender by a skill position player.

Wide: A defensive front with the tackles in a 41 alignment.

Win: A pass rush game with the weak inside defender having contain.

Y

Y: A tight end.

Z

0 Alignment: A head-up alignment on the center; a head-up alignment on another offensive lineman will be tagged with their position; for example: 0 alignment on the guard.

Zip: A 3 technique away from the call.

About the Author

Kenny Ratledge is the defensive coordinator at Sevier County High School (6A) in Sevierville, Tennessee. Ratledge has had numerous football articles published in national publications as well as authoring four books, *Attacking Football's Wing-T*, *Football's Attacking 46 Defense*, *Coaching Football's Special Teams*, and *Developing a Defensive Game Plan*.

Ratledge previously coached at Doyle High School in Knoxville, Tennessee, and Lenoir City High School in Tennessee. A defensive coordinator for 30 years, Ratledge has coached defensive line, inside linebackers, outside linebackers, secondary, offensive line, and special teams. During his career he has also coached track, baseball, and basketball.

In 1997, Ratledge's Sevier County team went to the state semifinals and led the state in scoring defense. The team won the state 5A championship in 1999, setting a state record with four interceptions in the championship game. Sevier County was the 2009 IMAC (Inter-Mountain Athletic Conference) champion, finishing the season 10-0. They had seven defenders on the all-conference team, with three defensive linemen making the first team. In 2010 Sevier County repeated as IMAC champions. The team had the best defense in their conference and finished fifth in scoring defense in the state. Sevier County led their conference in both rushing and passing defense. Sevier County gave up an average of eleven points per game (the varsity gave up only six points per game). The team's defense forced twenty-four turnovers and scored four defensive touchdowns. In addition, five members of the 2010 defense made first team all-conference, including both defensive tackles and both defensive ends made second team all-conference.

A graduate of the University of Tennessee (BS, MS), Ratledge earned an Ed.S. degree from Lincoln Memorial University. He has also attained a professional teaching rating of Career Ladder Level III (highest level). In 2002, was named the AFLAC National Assistant Coach of the Year.